Command and Combat Use of Combined Arms

(GERMAN FIELD SERVICE REGULATIONS)

SEPTEMBER 1, 1921.

Germany. Reichswehrministerium

The Naval & Military Press Ltd

*Published by*

**The Naval & Military Press Ltd**

Unit 5 Riverside, Brambleside
Bellbrook Industrial Estate
Uckfield, East Sussex
TN22 1QQ England

Tel: +44 (0)1825 749494

www.naval-military-press.com
www.nmarchive.com

Ministry of National Defense
Chief of Staff
No. 1/9, 21 T. 4, 1

Berlin, 1. September 1921

The regulations "Command and Combat Use of Combined Arms" applicable to all arms, are hereby issued.

These regulations are based on the strength, armament, and equipment of an army of a modern military Power, and not on the German Army of 100,000 men formed in accordance with the provisions of the treaty of peace.

Only by keeping alive the memory of the combat arms of which we are now deprived (air service, heavy artillery, tanks, etc.) will we be able to find means and ways of conducting a battle against an enemy with modern equipment. The lack of these arms must not lead to timidity in the attack. Their place can be partly filled by great mobility, good training, skill in the utilization of terrain, and frequent night operations. Troops must learn to evade hostile aerial observation. In maneuvers one side is frequently without modern combat arms, and the other side is assumed to have them.

The greatest emphasis must be placed upon the cooperation of all arms, from the smallest units up, especially the infantry and artillery.

# #

#

These regulations are issued for the purpose of offering to commanders and troops a uniform training based on the experiences of the War.

The missing chapters and the appendix will be published as soon as compiled.

von Seeckt.

ms

# TABLE OF CONTENTS.



mn

me

# I. COMMAND AND ITS MEANS.

## A. Organization and Distribution of Troop Units.

1. The organization of troop units governs the command and supply of the army in the field. This organization is prescribed by the General Staff and can be changed only by it.

2. The field armies of the large military powers consist of armies, several of which can be united into army groups.

Armies are composed of army corps or separate divisions, as well as army troops directly under the command of armies, (such as tanks, air service, artillery, engineers, signal corps, motor transport, supply units, etc.)

Army corps are composed of two or more divisions and the corps troops under the immediate orders of the corps, (same as above under armies).

Cavalry divisions are under the direct orders of general headquarters or army groups, seldom under orders of armies. Several cavalry divisions may be combined into a cavalry corps under a higher cavalry commander.

For aerial operations, strong air service units are organized into larger units, as attack, bombing, and pursuit squadrons.

The general reserves are under the direct orders of general headquarters. They consist of army corps or divisions, cavalry divisions, aviation, trench mortars, artillery, tanks, engineers, and special troops. They are attached to the different army groups or armies as needed.

The division and the cavalry division are the combat units. They contain within themselves all means necessary for independent operations. But frequently occasions arise, when it is necessary to reinforce the division or cavalry division. The troops attached in these circumstances are placed under the immediate orders of the division commander.

3. The distribution of the troops gives the temporary arrangement for certain operations and for tactical purposes (such as advance guard, main body, flank guard, combat groups, etc.) Units are broken up as little as possible.

## B. Command.

4. Command is divided into higher, middle, and lower. Higher command includes the command of units down to army corps and cavalry corps; middle command includes the command of divisions and cavalry divisions; lower command includes the command of all other units.

Any commander, leading an independent mixed detachment, is called the commander of the troops.

ms

5. The commander must possess the confidence and the respect of his troops. He must possess a strong will and an upright character as well as knowledge and ability. Hard and fast rules, suitable for all contingencies, cannot be laid down for his tactical movements; they would lead to one-sidedness, which is opposed to the manifold phases of warfare. Clear reasons must guide the commander. He must adhere to them in the face of the enemy, especially at the critical phases of combat.

The principal fingermark of a leader is his willingness to assume responsibility. All commanders always remember, and so teach their subordinates, that negligence and omission are more serious faults than errors in the choice of means.

Personal touch with the troops intrusted to them is of special importance to commanders of all ranks. In this way they are able from personal observation, to estimate correctly the needs and the capacity of their troops. When troops know that their commander lives for them and shares their trials and sufferings, they are willing to expend their last bit of strength to attain success, and will also endure defeat. The true inner value of troops, from the commander down to the last private, is shown only in reverses.

6. The mission and the situation form the basis for leadership.

7. The mission indicates the object to be attained. The commander never loses sight of it.

8. The situation seldom is so clear as to give complete insight into the enemy's conditions. Uncertainty in war is the rule. However, an alert and efficient commander frequently perceives important indications from small bits of information. Correct interpretation of these and the ability to exploit them with decision, is the basis of success.

9. The decision is based on the mission and the situation. When the mission no longer suffices as a basis for action and is superceded by events, this fact is considered in making the decision.

The commander bears the full responsibility when he does not execute a mission or when he changes it. When doing so, he must act in accordance with the general plan.

The decision must always be a whole-hearted one. Victory is won only by the will to win.

A decision once arrived at should never be changed without the best of reasons. But when the combat situation changes rapidly, rigid adherence to the decision can also be faulty. It is an art of leadership to determine when a new decision must be made.

10. The attack alone lays down the law to the enemy. The superiority of commander and troops is best shown by it. It is especially effective to envelope one or both hostile wings and attack the enemy's rear. Through such action the enemy can be annihilated.

All orders for attack must bear the mark of the greatest deci-

ms

sion. The will to conquer on the part of the commander must be shared by the last private.

The main force is always placed at the decisive point. Therefore, the troops are distributed in the beginning with this in mind. Thus every attack is given its center of gravity. This is especially emphasized in orders.

If, during a battle, success is attained at a point other than where intended, it is fully exploited there.

11. The fruits of victory are gathered in the pursuit. Pursuit aims at the annihilation of the enemy where that was impossible in the preceding combat. Measures for pursuit are taken early, so troops that are still available can be started in the decisive direction. Action on the flank and rear of the enemy is sought always. Exhaustion of the troops is never an excuse for abandoning pursuit entirely or partially. The last breath of man and horse is relentlessly used, and the last airplane sacrificed, if necessary to prevent the enemy from making a renewed stand. The utmost intrepidity is necessary. Only in this way are additional sacrifices in a renewed battle avoided.

12. Defense is justifiable only against a greatly superior enemy and for making possible an attack at some other place or at a later time. We must demand of troops, resistance and sacrifice to the last man. The defender utilizes the terrain as much as possible without, however, endangering the tactical cooperation with troops attacking at some other point.

Fortification of the terrain gives the defense additional strength which may offset even great hostile numerical superiority.

But the defender is more uncertain concerning the opponent's intentions than is the attacker. Reconnaissance and observation by all available means and holding out strong reserves are necessary in order to take timely counter-measures.

Troops are distributed in accordance with the purpose of the combat. Deception, varying the strength of the sectors, and great mobility of all reserves, are important means of attaining the greatest resistance and of breaking up the hostile attacking troops. Even with inferior numerical strength the defender strives to finish the battle with the offensive by striking the enemy a decisive blow.

13. A delaying action should deceive the enemy, hold him, and gain time. Whether the method used is the offensive or the defensive, depends on circumstances. It is the duty of the commander to avoid a decisive battle. On a wide front, large detachments are frequently used for delaying actions. In such cases, it is advisable to fortify the terrain.

14. The decision to break off a battle, either to retreat or to withdraw, is made by the commander only after he has exhausted all possibilities of victory, or when the battle is to be resumed under more favorable conditions at another point. To decide this matter at the correct moment is one of the most important duties of the commander.

ms

Only extreme necessity justifies withdrawal from battle. If withdrawal is necessary, distance is gained from the enemy as rapidly as possible. It is the duty of the higher commander to lead the movement in confidence; it is the duty of all subordinate commanders to keep up the morale of the troops by all means.

15. It is an art to concentrate all available forces for the decisive stroke. Numerical inferiority is offset by greater mobility. In this matter, the marching capacity of the troops plays a great role, as well as the use of railroads, trucks, and vehicles of all kinds, and darkness for concealing movements.

Frequently the commander must be satisfied with a force that appears numerically insufficient. This requires economy of forces at non-decisive points.

When advancing in several columns, the general rule to march to the sound of the cannons and to strive for union with neighbors, is not always the correct procedure. We should far rather carefully consider whether adherence to the original march direction and accomplishments of assigned missions would not lead to greater success.

16. The extension of the troops in line depends on the mission, supports, and on the terrain. It is restricted by the amount and kind of flank protection. When a unit has only one flank protected or is fighting independently, the extension is governed by our intentions and the conduct of the enemy. It differs in attack and defense. When the terrain is favorable and especially when it has been fortified, broad fronts are permissible. Troops frequently fight in groups. If the extension is too great there is danger of penetration, if the extension is too limited there is danger of being enveloped or turned. But frequently the prerequisite for success lies in great extension. Judgment on the part of the commander determines the proper extension.

The purpose of the battle is the principal factor governing the distribution of the troops. Every decisive battle requires distribution in depth and the holding of reserves in readiness.

17. Every commander possesses effective means of influencing the course of a battle in his unexpended forces, namely his reserve. In it, he has a means to shift the center of gravity to any desired point and to furnish support where he deems it necessary. The mobility of the reserve is increased by the use of motor trucks.

The determination of strength, location, and the use of the reserve require careful consideration. To weaken the fighting troops in order to build up the reserve often endangers success and exposes ourselves to defeat in detail. There are cases when it is better for one or another subordinate commander to do without a reserve.

The reserve in the form of mixed units must be capable of performing independent duties in battle. Disrupting units is undesirable.

The location of the reserve depends on our intentions and on the terrain. Its location must assure timely envelopment of the enemy

ms

or protection of our flank. If placed on the flank, the reserve is echeloned. Distance and intervals increase with the strength of the echelons.

Keeping the reserve far in rear saves its powers; keeping it close to the fighting line hastens its interference. The clearer the commander is, in his own mind, reference the employment of the reserve, and the nearer the time for its employment comes, the closer he moves his reserve to the fighting troops.

When launching his reserves, the commander loses his most effective means of influencing the course of the battle. But in spite of this fact, he must not hesitate, if thereby is success. On the other hand, he never prematurely uses his reserves because his subordinates plead for support.

When reserves have been thrown into the fight, the commander at once strives to form a new reserve from troops on less important fronts.

## C. INFORMATION AND REPORTS

### Situation Map.

18. Information and reports received of the enemy form an important basis for the estimate of the situation and execution of the decision. All information and the very best reports lose their value if they arrive too late. Therefore means are provided for rapid transmission of reports. Frequently the espionage service and statements of the enemy's press give us the first clue as to the enemy. Aerial and ground reconnaissance give us more detailed information of the enemy. This reconnaissance consists in seeking out and maintaining continuous observation of the enemy. Accurate conclusions can generally be drawn from the sum total of reports from the various sources. Even apparently insignificant details may acquire importance when considered in connection with other information.

19. Within his zone of action, every commander carries on continuous day and night reconnaissance of the enemy. Contact with the enemy once gained is never lost. All information received is transmitted without delay to the next higher commander, adjacent units and one's own troops.

20. Listening-in on hostile telegraph, telephone lines, and wireless, noting statements of inhabitants, scrutinizing captured mail, documents and telegrams, capturing airplanes, balloons, automobiles, carrier-pigeons, and messenger dogs, supplements direct observation of the enemy.

21. Statements of prisoners are especially important, as well as papers found on killed or prisoners, in villages, positions, vehicles, tanks, airplanes, and balloons.

All prisoners, after brief interrogation, and all documents, after scrutiny, are immediately transmitted to the commander; they are never held by the troops. Clever and rapid interrogation of individual prisoners is of great importance. It is important that the commander learn from prisoners, the composition and location of the enemy's units and those adjacent, organizations, names of commanders, their last station, marches, railroad journeys, condition and morale of the hostile troops, and missions assigned.

ms

If it is impracticable to immediately interrogate prisoners, then at least names and numbers of troop units are ascertained.

22. At each higher headquarters, one officer is detailed to collate the reconnaissance reports and other information received, and to direct counter espionage.

23. In drawing up reports, a distinction is made between what the observer has seen personally, what some one else has said or seen, and what is merely suspected. The source of information is stated, and reasons given for suspicions.

24. Numbers, time, and place are stated exactly.

It is of great importance for the command to know where nothing has been seen of the enemy. Equally valuable is a statement confirming previous reports, or a statement that conditions have not changed during a definite period.

Remarks on condition of terrain are always appended to reports. This must not be omitted in the mutual exchange of information between infantry and artillery.

25. It is important that reports make clear the situation and give the commander a good basis for his decision. Their number is unimportant. Therefore, careful consideration is given each bit of information concerning the enemy, as to whether it should be immediately reported or reported at all. Useless reports increase the difficulties of the commander, burden the means of communications, and delay transmission of other reports. First contact with the enemy is always reported. Reports, which exaggerate the results of reconnaissance, our successes or those of the enemy are always dangerous and frequently even fatal. Clear and concise reports drawn up without assumptions and exaggeration, show strength of character and tactical understanding on the part of the writer.

Supplementing or confirmation of reports by observation from elevated points and aerial photographs is always of special value.

26. Combat furnishes the most reliable information of the enemy. Good communication between command posts and between commanders and troops in combat is therefore necessary.

27. During combat, reports of the situation are sent continuously. To accomplish this, pauses in fighting and approach of darkness must be utilized. At the end of a battle, a final report on the outcome, the condition of our troops, and that of the enemy is submitted.

28. In urgent cases, reports are submitted directly to the commander of the troops and the next superior commander. Troops threatened by the enemy are informed of that fact immediately. Every report contains a notation, enumerating the command posts to which it has been sent.

29. All information and reports must be correctly evaluated. There is always an inclination to obtain from reports just what we desire. Reports that come direct from the battlefield are frequently exaggerated.

ms

30. At each headquarters, a suitably trained officer is charged with preparing a situation map and keeping it up to date. This gives the commander a complete grasp of the situation, shows him the course of events, and facilitates the making of decisions. The situation of neighboring troops is also indicated thereon.

D. ESTIMATE OF THE SITUATION, DECISION

31. In considering our own situation, we first determine what action is required by the mission, where the different portions of our troops are located, what forces are immediately available for executing the mission, and what forces are available later. Possibility of support by neighboring troops, as well as supporting them, are considered. Results so far accomplished and condition of the troops is considered; when the situation is tense, however, these considerations withdraw to the background. Use of railroads and motor trucks for movement of troops are given careful consideration.

32. The estimate of the enemy's situation must not lead to biased opinion. Based on reports and information received, we must consider what measures the enemy will take to oppose the execution of our mission. Though we can never know what decision the enemy has made, we will do well to assume that he will act tactically correct.

We should principally consider: What localities and what line can the enemy have reached? Are there any indications of his strength and disposition? In what direction may the enemy continue his movements? What measures will he probably take? What is the condition of his railroads and roads? The peculiarities of the hostile commander and his troops may indicate his probable action.

33. A knowledge of and a correct estimate of the terrain have a very great influence on the measures to be taken.

34. The logical result of all considerations must be a firm decision. Waiting for further information is seldom a sign of will power on the part of the commander and easily becomes a grave error.

E. ORDERS.

35. The decision is transformed into action through orders. Orders express the will of the commander and state the duties of the subordinate commanders clearly, concisely, and without ambiguity. Orders must not interfere with the subordinate commanders in the independent execution of them.

36. In all orders clearness supercedes correct form. The one issuing the orders places himself in the position of the recipient in order to determine how he would act in the premises and what misunderstandings are possible. He further ascertains how long it will take the order to reach all subordinates.

Meaningless expressions are avoided, such as, "if possible", "under certain conditions", "oppose", "lay hands on a certain place", "attempt to". They only lead to half-measures. Exaggerations like "urgent", "absolutely", "without resting", "energetically", etc are also avoided. They soon lose force and no attention is paid to them.

me

Assumptions and expectations seldom belong in orders, reasons, never.

37. Orders are generally devoid of details, especially when changes in the situation are probable or possible before the orders can be executed. This should specially be remembered when drawing up large scale orders, covering several day's operations. In such cases, only the plan, the objective to be reached, and some directions for execution are sufficient. In such cases, instructions take the place of orders.

38. As a general rule, the regimental commander issues written orders: the higher and medium commanders invariably do. Simple directions and short tasks may be given verbally or by telephone. But they are recorded in writing at once.

All other lower commanders issue written orders in cases only when verbal or mechanical transmission is impossible or objectionable because the enemy may listen-in.

In important cases, acknowledgement of receipt and literal repetition is required. Orders, when transmitted by wireless, are generally in code; when transmitted by telephone, they are in code only when there is danger of listening-in.

39. It is generally not advisable to transmit the entire orders received from higher headquarters with additions. It is better for each headquarters to issue its own orders, especially in open situations.

40. Combat orders regulate the combat activities of the troops in the field. They are headed with the designation of the headquarters issuing them, (army, corps, division, artillery, regimental orders, etc.), or according to tactical units (advance guard, outpost, orders, etc.)

41. It is recommended that combat orders be arranged in the following sequence:

Information of the enemy, information of neighboring troops, as far as the recipient should know;
Plan of the commander;
Reconnaissance;
Missions assigned the different units noted in the "distribution of troops";
Location of the commander;
A notation is added to whom and how the orders are issued.

Under "troops", which is written on the left of the body of the order, the troop units are mentioned by arms within tactical groups, as follows: infantry, special machine gun, cyclist, trench mortar, tank, air service, cavalry, artillery, including observation and anti-aircraft units, light ammunition columns, engineers including bridge trains and searchlight platoons, signal corps troops, sanitary troops, motor transport troops and trains. If the march sequence is prescribed, the troops are mentioned accordingly. Then in the heading above "troop" appears, "in order of march", (advance guard, main body, rearguard, etc.)

In marching to the rear, the order of march of troops is always given.

ms

42. Frequently, combat orders are preceded by warning orders which contain for example, plan of the commander, instructions reference reconnaissance, place and hour of departure, subsequent march objective or location of shelter, security troops, security lines. The subordinate commander then is able to make preparatory arrangements. The warning orders are for the purpose of sparing the troops and therefore avoid unnecessary alarm and premature preparation.

43. Frequently the urgency of the situation requires the issuance of special orders to one or more units. But this method has the disadvantage of including only a portion of the command. Special orders contain the most necessary details concerning activity and mission of the other arms, especially of the infantry and artillery, as otherwise there can be no cooperation between the arms. Complete combat orders follow as a rule.

44. Combat orders are free from a fixed outline. They are also issued as complete orders. The troops are mentioned therein according to the march sequence, or, if already developed and deployed, from the right flank.

45. Special instructions in combat orders for the separate units or for all units, contain details for reconnaissance and collection of information, for aerial protection, for connection between headquarters and troops. They further regulate the movements of the combat trains, field trains, replenishment of ammunition, subsistence, medical and veterinary service, as well as technical measures for automobile traffic (fuel, tools, and repairs for all units that have motor vehicles). In simpler or smaller units, these directions are included in the combat orders.

Special instructions for supply trains regulate their activities in detail, for example, distribution of trains, missions of the single sections and trains not belonging to a definite headquarters, replenishment of emptied trains. In general, they are issued only to the units which they concern. As these units do not generally receive the combat orders for the sake of secrecy, extracts of the necessary details are furnished.

46. Orders of the day, (corps, division) treat of administration of the interior; routine reports and personnel matters, etc.

Staff orders regulate the administration at higher headquarters.

## F. TRANSMISSION OF ORDERS AND REPORTS.

47. Transmission of orders is made through military channels. Only in urgent cases are orders ever issued to a unit, otherwise than through military channels; intermediate commands that have been skipped, are notified as soon as possible.

48. For transmission of orders and reports, there are first, the technical means available. Transmission through the main instrument, the telephone, is expedited when an officer is at each end.

ms

Transmission by persons or relay stations is necessary when technical means are lacking or when they fail. In doubtful cases, do not hesitate to use them.

49. Important orders, reports and messages are sent by officers conversant with the situation, frequently by means of automobiles and airplanes.

50. In all other cases, written orders and reports are sent by mounted messengers, cyclists, motorcyclists, and runners. Specially brave and tried men are employed in carrying orders under fire. Messenger dogs and carrier pigeons also are used.

51. In less important cases, every man carrying an order or report should know its contents; every mounted messenger, in so far as secrecy will allow should know the contents of the report he carries. As soon as contact with the enemy or hostile populace is imminent, officers are sent, accompanied by mounted messengers or guards, and in such cases single messengers are not sent. It will often be advisable to transmit orders in duplicate along different routes and by different means, and to use armored cars.

52. The sender carefully designates the route to be taken and explains it. Names of places are written as on the map and also phonetically. When mounted messengers meet officers, they do not slacken the prescribed speed, they give their names and name of headquarters for whom they carry orders. The mounted messengers always have the right of way. It is the duty of every officer to assist them. All commanders from the regimental commander upwards and the leader of a reconnaissance detachment are privileged to read messages and orders passing them. Exercise of this privilege is noted over their signature on the orders or reports.

53. To simplify transmission of reports and to shorten the routes, headquarters frequently establish message centers in the direction of the strongest traffic, which take over the further transmission of all reports, etc., coming from or going to the troops. These message centers must be easy to find, must be outside the hostile fire zone, and must be securely connected with their headquarters for the transmission of all reports. Their location is timely divulged to the troops.

Under special conditions, for example, with cavalry divisions operating independently, message centers are established far to the front. They have the same duties as all other message centers, to simplify the transmission of messages and to shorten the route between reconnoitering detachments and cavalry division. Messages received are collected, examined, and condensed. In addition the messages may be coded there. These message centers generally transmit messages etc. by the technical means, (telephone lines, wireless, airplanes, automobiles, etc.) seldom by other means. They require extensive protection and are commanded by specially selected officers who are familiar with the commander's plans.

Dropping grounds for airplanes are established on the march, during halts, in shelter, and in battle as close to the commander as prac-

ms

ticable, and must be plainly marked by identification panels. These should have means of communication.

## G. COMMUNICATION BETWEEN HEADQUARTERS.

54. A prerequisite to successful command, is a well established, rapidly and reliably working communication service. It assures cooperation of all units in the execution of a definite task and specially assures cooperation of all arms in battle. Establishment of this communication service and, principally its protection from hostile fire, demand very thorough preparation.

55. While at rest, on the march, and in battle, every command post establishes communication by technical means with the command post of the next smaller unit and maintains it. Only exceptionally, according to circumstances in each case, may the higher commander direct a contrary or mixed procedure in this regard.

Subordinate command posts do everything to establish and maintain communication with the next higher command post. It is a mistake to wait for establishment of new communications or repair of destroyed communications.

Technical communication with adjacent units, during the continual changes in open warfare, is accomplished quickest by the common superior commander; independently of this, however, each unit establishes communication with the neighbor on its right.

In stabilized situations permanent communication between all neighboring units is required. It is made from left to right.

56. Existing communications with neighboring troops must never lead to mutual dependence nor weaken one's own power of action. Mutual cooperation and the best connection is generally best assured by all units relentlessly pushing forward.

57. Communication between infantry and artillery is of the utmost importance. When that fails, the entire action may become endangered. It is the duty of the artillery to establish and maintain communication with the infantry. This duty is performed by keeping close to the sister arm, by maintaining its own observation, and through rapid and mostly independent action, which meets the desires and requirements of the infantry.

The infantry also promotes communication between the two arms by every possible means, such as flares from its leading companies and infantry airplanes. This, in order to supplement the observation of the artillery and to communicate to the latter its wishes.

58. The staff officer of the signal corps troops at division headquarters designates the lines to be established for the communication system within the division. He is always informed of the situation and the plans of the commander, so that he may timely construct his lines of communication.

The signal officers of the various units keep in close touch

ms

with the division signal officer, and supervise the entire service of communication of their units in accordance with instructions from their immediate commanders.

59. Command posts and shelters for headquarters are plainly marked day and night, with due precautions against aerial observation; the same measures are taken reference telephone stations, message centers, and the roads leading thereto. Special guidons are designated for headquarters from regimental headquarters up.

60. The telephone is the most important technical means of communication and forms the basis for the communication system; consequently, the establishment of the network of lines should receive great importance. In open situations, the commander must be satisfied with a simple net; in stabilized situations, the construction is made with all means at hand. As a rule two lines run both ways from all headquarters.

Rapid telegraphy and telautographs are used only at higher headquarters (general headquarters, army groups, armies, corps).

Wireless is a valuable supplement to the telephone. It principally serves to bridge wide spaces, but performs valuable service even in smaller units because of its rapid working and slight sensitiveness to the effects of hostile fire. Brevity is necessary, however, in sending messages by wireless. It is forbidden to send important decisions and orders by wireless, as there is danger that even messages in code may be deciphered by the enemy in a short time.

Airplanes are an excellent means of communication for bridging great distances. For this reason they are specially suited for communication between the higher headquarters. And during close or battle reconnaissance, they are a reliable means of communication between commander and troops. Fog precludes their employment; darkness limits it.

In addition, the following means can be used to close gaps in the network of communication; balloons, wireless telephones, ground telegraphy, visual signals, sound and light signals, information bombs, pigeons, messenger dogs, runners, relays, mounted messengers and liaison officers.

Carrier pigeons and messenger dogs are principally employed for communicating with the troops in the foremost lines when all other means fail. Darkness and fog forbid the use of pigeons.

One always considers what messages should be coded, and what messages cannot be sent by certain means, because by the use of those means the enemy may pick them up.

## H. LOCATION OF THE COMMANDER

61. Possibility of rapid and permanent establishment of a communication system is an important factor in the selection of the command posts of the higher commanders. But they cannot rely absolutely on technical means of communication.

ms

Remaining too far in rear delays transmission of orders and instructions in spite of the improvements in technical means of communication, and leads to the loss or delayed arrival of orders and messages.

And, if the commander of a large force is too far in rear, difficulties of personal influence on the troops are increased. And this is of great importance. At decisive moments, troops like to see their commander; the same as in times of rest, they appreciate his personal efforts for their welfare.

And, finally, too great a distance in rear deprives the commander and his staff of personal knowledge concerning the peculiarity of the terrain.

The commander is always where he can be found. The business of his office demands quietness. This requires the location to be as permanent as possible. This permanency can be safeguarded even during a rapid advance considering the means at hand for quick transportation. By these means, he is enabled to overtake in a few hours, his troops which have marched for several days.

62. The division commander is always in the midst of his troops. During an advance, his place is well to the front; when the division marches in several columns, his place is with the main column.

When contact is made with the enemy, it is best for the division commander to have personal observation.

In order not to attract the enemy's attention, the division staff advances in echelons; a portion thereof is generally left back at a previously designated place, when necessary.

When directing the battle, the division commander occupies his command post. This station is as far to the front as practicable and still so located that the lines of communication to the flank and rear are beyond effective hostile fire. It is desirable to have a commanding view of the battlefield from the command post. If this is impracticable, observation officers from division headquarters are stationed at prominent points, closer to or farther away from the battlefield. The artillery commander arranges to locate his command post near the command post of division headquarters.

At the command post care must be taken - through strict discipline and by keeping away all persons that have no business there - to allow the division commander to work in tranquility and to prevent his attention from being distracted by minor details. Frequent changes of division headquarters are avoided. Change of command post is made only after communication at the new command post has been established; otherwise reports and messages may not reach the division commander at the time when an important decision must be made. Proper arrangements are made for forwarding reports, etc., which reach the abandoned command post.

63. Lower commanders must be close to their troops for reasons of morale; also because they must have a good view of the terrain, personal observation of the enemy, and in addition, must have good communication

ms

with the next higher commander. The lower commanders change their command post according to the progress of the battle, so that their personal influence on the conduct of the troops is always assured. They frequently locate their command post near their reserves.

I It is well to combine the command post of the infantry and artillery commanders, engaged in the same sector, or at least, locate them very close to each other, for closer cooperation. This is always striven for, but the direct influence of the commander over his troops takes priority.

64. In the pursuit, the place of all commanders is well forward. Their appearance in front spurs the troops to renewed efforts and gives them the power necessary to hold positions gained, and to fully exploit the victory.

65. In the retreat, the highest commander with his artillery commander proceeds to the point where the next resistance is to be offered, only after the former is convinced that his orders for the retreat have reached the last unit. During the retreat all subordinate commanders remain with their units.

## J. THE STAFF OF THE COMMANDER.

66. Correct organization of the staff, and proper distribution of the work among the members according to their ability, knowledge, and energy, is of great importance.

It is absolutely necessary for the chief of staff to enjoy the absolute confidence of the commander and of the troops.

ms

## II. AIR SERVICE AND CAVALRY

### A. AIR SERVICE.

67. The air service is divided into observation units and combat units.

68. The observation squadrons assigned to armies, corps and divisions and occasionally to army groups and general headquarters, are charged with making distant and battle reconnaissance, supporting the infantry and artillery on the march and on the battlefield (infantry and artillery planes), as well as serving for communication and courier purposes. They are employed singly or in formations of 2 to 3 planes, (for aerial reconnaissance see Part III);

69. Attack, bombing, and pursuit squadrons comprise the aerial combat force. Differing from the observation squadrons, they operate as a general rule in close order as combat units; they are generally under the direct orders of the higher commanders. The number of aerial combat units attached to an army or army group varies according to the situation.

70. The squadron is the unit of all aerial forces. While the general rule obtains, to place the artillery flights of the observation squadrons under the tactical orders of the artillery commander, the squadron unit of combat squadrons is never disrupted.

71. Aerial combat forces are a powerful weapon in the hands of the commander; their employment is regulated by strict orders.

Ready for early employment at the frontier, the aerial combat forces, organized into strong units, give the commander the power of exerting a material influence on the hostile measures even during the period of concentration. During operations, it is the duty of the commander to direct aerial reconnaissance in the proper direction, and to concentrate superior aerial combat forces for cooperation with the other arms in the decisive battle. For this purpose, all available airplanes are used; troop units that do not directly participate in the decision, generally do without aerial support.

72. Attack squadrons are used to attack ground targets with machine guns and bombs. The appearance of planes, flying in close order at low altitude above marching, fighting, or resting troops, produces a great moral and material effect on friend and foe. They are not suited for the destruction of strong objects by bombing, such as bridges.

73. During the approach march and in the pursuit, attack squadrons are used against the main bodies of the hostile columns. Their effect is increased if they succeed in attacking the enemy when he is crossing a defile. Troops marching in close order or resting, especially cavalry, are very sensitive to aerial attacks. Surprise attacks on airdromes, unprotected bivouacs, troops detraining, are always accompanied by great success. In our own retreat, the attack squadrons stop the hostile marching columns that are the most dangerous.

ms

74. Attack squadrons are most useful in the battle. They must be in the best of condition for this work.

Good objectives within the zone of infantry defense are found, only if the enemy bases his defense on plainly visible portions of the terrain (clumps of woods, edges of villages, etc.) In such cases the attack squadrons are launched simultaneously with the infantry assault on those points where the center of gravity of the assault lies and where the hostile resistance is to be broken quickly. If, in defense, the hostile assaulting infantry is observed in readiness, then the use of attack squadrons in close order can weaken the force of the hostile assault, delay it, or even stop it completely.

But the objectives of the attack squadrons are generally farther in rear, for example, hostile reserves, battery nests, strong points, and supply trains. In the defense, it may be better to hold attack squadrons in readiness for counterattacks, instead of throwing them into the oscillating infantry fighting.

By using the attack squadrons as units at the decisive point, and by assigning them a definite mission, dispersion is avoided.

75. Bombing squadrons supplement the work of the attack squadrons. The greater carrying capacity of these planes gives effect to their bombing attack; their greater cruising radius enables them to be employed against objectives far in rear of the hostile front. They are generally employed against targets that are beyond the effective range of our artillery and for destructive work. But bombing squadrons are not suited for repelling hostile aerial combat forces; therefore their employment is generally limited to work at night.

The commander uses the bombing squadrons in a systematic way and avoids dispersion of effect, by attacking a few targets at one time.

76. During forward movements, bombing attacks are directed principally against hostile detraining stations and shelters. Shortly prior to contact, the hostile airdromes and various headquarters become the most important objectives.

During battle and in the pursuit, the main task of the bombing squadrons is to prevent the movement of troops by rail and to interfere with all railroad traffic; and therefore, bombing squadrons are principally employed against the entraining stations of the enemy that have been located. In our own retreat, bombing attacks are directed against the hostile railheads where the opponent is forced to store his ammunition, subsistence and all other supplies.

Bombing squadrons are also useful in stabilized situations. Carefully planned bombing attacks materially aid our own attack and delay the hostile attack preparations.

77. Fighting to gain supremacy of the air starts principally in the endeavor to assure our own aerial reconnaissance, to prevent that of the enemy, and to protect our troops, works and population from aerial attacks. Numerous pursuit squadrons are concentrated to gain the supremacy of the air.

ms

The battle for supremacy of the air is carried on offensively. The hostile aerial force is sought out and attacked beyond our lines. The opponent is forced to take the defensive and his strength and initiative broken by destroying as many of his airplanes as possible.

Considering the peculiarities of aerial fighting, it is impossible to screen or blockade a certain sector by defensive tactics.

Even strong aerial superiority cannot permanently stop hostile aerial activity, but can merely weaken and limit it. For this reason, measures are taken on the ground to increase the difficulties of hostile aerial reconnaissance.

78. During concentration and at the beginning of war, aerial reconnaissance is assured by employing pursuit squadrons. Single, long distance reconnaissance airplanes require no support by pursuit squadrons as a general rule. The battle activities of the pursuit squadrons are transferred to points where the commander desires to gain detailed information. The activities of pursuit and observation squadrons are coordinated. After our aerial reconnaissance is assured, surplus pursuit squadrons are employed where it is desirable to prevent the enemy from gaining information.

79. During the battle, the hostile artillery airplanes and captive balloons are the most important objectives for our pursuit squadrons. By continually repeated advances to the line of the hostile artillery, our planes attempt to destroy the airplanes directing the fire of the hostile artillery. Frequent attacks against balloons, even if they do not destroy the balloons, increase the difficulties of hostile observation.

Where the decisive attack is being made, the hostile aerial fighting forces are driven off by waves of our pursuit squadrons. During the progress of the attack on the ground, the battlefield is watched and our infantry and artillery protected against hostile planes. In defense, the main forces are held back until the hostile infantry attack is launched. The masses of hostile planes which appear then, are met by equal or superior aerial forces.

## B. INDEPENDENT CAVALRY

80. Besides reconnaissance, the great strategical and tactical importance of cavalry lies in its ability to concentrate rapidly a strong fire power against the sensitive points of the enemy. This ability is based on high mobility, ample equipment with fire arms of all kinds, and ammunition for them. (Concerning reconnaissance activities of cavalry see Part III.)

81. Effect of firearms precludes mounted fighting in larger commands. In small commands, cavalry detachments use the mounted attack at favorable opportunities, for example, against fleeing hostile infantry or when encountering hostile cavalry by surprise.

82. Cavalry is under orders of general headquarters or army group headquarters, seldom under army headquarters. Assignment of cavalry to a corps or a division is exceptional, and is done only when needed for

purely tactical duties in close cooperation with infantry.

83. Offensive screening of our own intentions, by driving back the hostile cavalry and preventing hostile cavalry reconnaissance, is always combined with strategical reconnaissance.

Defensive screening is considered only occasionally, and when specially favorable terrain conditions exist, (stream sectors).

84. Cavalry is employed on an extensive front till the arrival of other troops. It is then, concentrated as soon as possible at the starting point for its strategical missions, so that this activity will not be delayed.

85. The commander-in-chief determines whether or not the hostile frontier guard shall be pierced.

If the advance of cavalry is stopped by terrain defended by the enemy or by fortifications, other troops with greater fighting power than the cavalry are rapidly employed to force a passage, the cavalry directly following it up or, the necessary infantry, artillery, etc. is attached to the cavalry.

It is always undesirable to weaken the fighting power of the cavalry by assigning it tasks such as breaking barriers, before starting it on its work proper.

86. When open situations obtain, the most important function of the cavalry besides strategical reconnaissance and driving the hostile cavalry from the field, is the envelopment of the hostile flanks.

This consists in operations against the enemy's flanks and rear. Depending on distance, this includes; holding down the hostile flanks, prevention of concentration and the bringing forward of hostile reinforcements, operations against hostile railroads and junction points (destructions), interference with hostile communications, and the hostile retreat (strategic pursuit).

87. Distant operations by large bodies of cavalry against the lines of communications in rear of the enemy, frequently offer a specially rich and paying field of activity. Prerequisite for this, is a liberal attachment of mobile auxiliary troops, (cyclists, infantry in motor trucks, artillery) plenty of ammunition, as well as leaving behind all unnecessary impediments. Only relentless advance and full utilization of the resources of the country (requisitioning of vehicles and subsistence) will lead to the objective.

It is the duty of the cavalry commander to take all necessary measures for keeping the less mobile arms up with the cavalry.

88. Besides its strategical work, the cavalry has many other duties which, in part, demand rather close communication with the army, viz: stopping the leading elements of the hostile army, protection of our flanks, establishing connection between two armies fighting separately, tactical employment on the flanks, security of broad sectors of the front which lie outside of the decisive area, investing fortresses, and finally, tactical pursuit and covering a retreat.

ms

89. Great success for the entire operation can be expected, only when the commander in chief allows the cavalry the necessary freedom of movements for its strategical action. Cavalry sent far to the front cannot be directed by orders from the rear. That cavalry never waits for them.

90. It is a mistake to employ the cavalry in front when there is no longer opportunities for cavalry action, for example, when the leading elements of opposing armies have gained contact. Then the cavalry has performed its mission and belongs, on a flank of the army, or in rear of the front as a mobile army reserve, unless urgent tactical necessity requires other dispositions.

91. When segeral cavalry divisions have been organized into a cavalry corps, the senior cavalry officer issues his orders as a rule, in the form of instructions; he leaves the method of execution to the cavalry divisions. However, designation of reconnaissance objectives, zones of action, and use of roads generally require more detailed orders.

92. The many duties of cavalry and the frequent and sudden changes in the situation demand that cavalry leaders possess special attributes. Good horsemanship, physical endurance, self-confidence, a sharp and trained eye, strategical and tactical knowledge, quick decision, and a firm will, as well as the gift to express his decision in clear, concise orders are these attributes. If possessed of these, he will clearly observe the proper moment for action and will then employ his troops with intrepidity. Deployment for battle and the start of an enveloping attack is always made mounted, in order to head off the enemy by our rapidity of movement.

93. All lower commanders are constantly informed of the general situation and plans of the commander.

94. Great importance must be attached to maintaining the fighting power and preservation of the valuable horses. The number and strength of the reconnaissance and security detachments corresponds to the strength of the cavalry unit in question. Exhaustion of the horses is avoided; halts for rests, feeding, and watering are properly timed. Unnecessary detours, useless losses, by movements in the open, or halting within the effective hostile fire zone are avoided. Cavalry should be saved, in order to demand the utmost from it at the decisive moment.

95. Because of aerial attacks, it will frequently be impossible for large units of cavalry to advance over open ground in day time. The columns either march at night or, in day time, are divided into smaller groups. Similarly, the ever present danger from aerial attack precludes large concentration of cavalry and the occupation of positions in readiness by large masses.

96. During halts, and when assembling for the march which is advantageously done in march groups with vehicles on the road, the detachments nearest the enemy and those on the flanks take over the security without waiting for special orders.

97. When road conditions permit, the cavalry division marches as a general rule in several columns, if possible by brigades. But it is necessary that the distance between the columns be such as to assure mutual cooperation.

me

1 98. Detachments having mobility and great fire power, such as; cyclists, heavy machine guns and artillery are attached to the advance guard for quickly overcoming weak resistance. In addition engineer detachments, armored automobiles, signal corps troops and radio stations are attached. The rule is to advance from line to line.

99. Frequently the infantry marches between the advance guard and the main body or, is sent ahead accompanied by one or more troops of cavalry, to be overtaken by the rest of the cavalry division in the course of the march. Detailed orders are necessary for this in order to avoid having the infantry enter combat prematurely and alone. The selection of lines of supply is important. Motor truck columns and requisitioned vehicles are employed for carrying the baggage.

100. It is always advisable to attach strong detachments of artillery and heavy machine guns to the rearguard. Smaller detachments with light machine guns march along parallel roads in order to surprise the enemy at every available opportunity by flanking fire. Preparations are made to hold the enemy for long periods, at every break in the terrain.

101. The advantage of mobility is realized most in the attack of the cavalry fighting alone or on the flank. Generally the fighting is done by separate groups mutually supporting each other; in this manner the enemy is attacked frontally by weak forces, while the main forces are sent against his flank and rear. Rapidity and surprise play a prominent role. The strength of each group, amount of infantry and artillery attached, depends on the importance of the mission. The main fire is concentrated at the decisive point.

1 102.. In the defense, especially when the situation is obscure, fighting by groups along an estensive front is also the rule. This method also serves to deceive the enemy. Here also, it is important that the groups mutually support each other by flanking fire and by holding out a small mobile reserve for attacking the enemy in flank. Thin connected lines lead to dispersion and are not suited for the purpose. The cavalry must have mobility even in defense.

103. The cavalry division is specially suited for conducting delaying actions even against a strongly superior enemy, and can do so either by attack or defense. The enemy is deceived along a broad front. In attack, the great mobility of the cavalry allows it to strike the enemy again and again at different places on flank; and in defense, advanced detachments which then can timely evade a superior enemy, can force the enemy to a premature deployment. Delaying actions are generally fought by groups.

104. Besides being able to fight on an extensive front, the cavalry is also able to conduct an attack or defense in a protracted space against an enemy equipped with all arms; and supported in depth. In this event, the front extension is made in accordance with the smaller number of carbines. In case of need, infantry, cyclists, light and heavy artillery, tanks, signal corps units, aerial fighting forces, etc. are attached.

105. After a battle is won, the pursuit of the enemy is the princi

ms

pal task of the cavalry. It is executed by all available forces.

106. It is the duty of every leader of an independent cavalry detachment to maintain contact with the enemy and to punish him as much as possible.

107. It will frequently be inadvisable to use the cavalry division as a unit for the tactical pursuit, but to assign definite tasks and objectives to the separate brigades and regiments which are reinforced by artillery.

108. Parallel pursuit is specially effective. Advancing along parallel roads, the cavalry attempts to overtake the hostile columns and repeatedly attack them in flank, to attack them with surprise fire, to push them off their line of retreat, to beat them to defiles, to destroy bridges in their front and to create confusion and panic in the midst of columns and trains. Armored motor cars are useful for this.

Parallel pursuit is carried out relentlessly and without regard to saving the troops, day and night, even with exhausted horses.

109. When the outcome of a battle is unfavorable, the cavalry facilitates the retreat of the other arms. In such a situation, the full utilization of mobility and attack against the flank of the pursuing enemy is frequently the best means. At other times, the pursuing enemy is forced to deploy by taking up broad rearguard positions, and taking full advantage of natural obstacles; and when the situation permits, the cavalry timely evades the enemy's attack and offers renewed resistance in another position.

110. The hostile pursuit is delayed by destroying bridges, blockading roads, cutting telegraph and telephone wire, etc.

111. Cavalry at rest does not, as a general rule, secure itself by a continuous outpost position. Detachments sent out to front and flanks reinforced under certain conditions by cyclists and machine guns which in turn send out patrols, secure the villages in front and the roads leading toward the enemy. Use of barricades is helpful. Arrangements for defense against aerial attacks are made. Avoid crowding cavalry into single villages, because of the probability of hostile aerial attacks. Protective measures to meet surprises are also taken in rear villages.

112. In camp or bivouac, the different arms are mingled. The nearer the enemy, the more the troops are crowded together and the more extensive are the preparations for meeting a hostile attack.

113. During hostile night attacks, the several villages are defended. Detailed instructions therefore are necessary.

114. Only in close proximity to the enemy is it advisable to carry out the service of security according to infantry methods. It may be advisable to establish an outpost with dismounted troops and to leave the horses with the resting troops.

ms

115. The cavalry can withdraw behind a natural division of the terrain for rest; the line to be held in case of hostile attack will then generally be along this division, provided terrain is not abandoned by the troops falling back, which will have to be retaken by fighting the next day. In the latter case, the security is kept in front of the natural division.

116. Only in stabilized situations and when both flanks are protected is it permissible to separate the cavalry from its horses by great distances and for a long period.

ms

# III. RECONNAISSANCE AND SECURITY

## A. RECONNAISSANCE IN GENERAL

117. Distant reconnaissance is the reconnaissance of distant objectives, the results of which form the basis for the decisions of the highest commander. Among other things, distant reconnaissance covers the hostile concentration and collection of supplies, railroad traffic, roads used, location of flying fields, construction of field railroads, permanent fortifications, direction of the enemy's advance, what march objectives he has reached, location of his flanks and rear echelons. This reconnaissance is performed by airplanes and by cavalry. However, all of the tasks cannot be performed by each of these arms. They are limited by their respective capabilities.

Army cavalry and airplanes supplement each other in performing distant reconnaissance. It is seldom possible for cavalry to gain a deep insight into hostile conditions, and therefore, this is generally the task of the airplanes. On the other hand, only cavalry can determine details, such as occupation of villages and woods, and can explore the terrain. Cavalry can also reconnoiter when airplane reconnaissance is stopped or interfered with by certain influences.

The reconnaissance made by either arm can never entirely take the place of that made by the other. Both arms can and do supplement each other. Frequently the results of aerial reconnaissance determine the proper direction in which the cavalry reconnaissance is made.

118. Close reconnaissance is principally for tactical purposes. It furnishes the commander with a proper basis for the tactical employment of his troops and enters into details. Some of these details are, for example: the location of points at which the leading elements of hostile columns were at a certain hour; determining the strength of different columns; the extent of hostile positions; details of those positions; details of detraining points, etc.

Close reconnaissance is performed mostly by airplanes, cavalry and cyclists, but is also performed independently by all other arms.

119. Battle reconnaissance includes the observation of all tactical measures taken by the enemy. This involves observing of the conduct of the enemy in and in rear of his front, locating his flanks, determining his artillery groupings, location and movements of his reserves, and the use made of reinforcements. Battle reconnaissance on our own flank is of special importance.

All arms participate in battle reconnaissance.

120. Distant and close reconnaissance overlap upon the close approach of the enemy. Close and battle reconnaissance overlap each other just prior to contact, and during battle they merge into each other.

121. Economy of men in all kinds of reconnaissance is advisable. It is not a question of the number of airplanes and patrols sent out, but rather that those sent out are daily informed concerning the situation and our plans, and that they are given clear missions from which the commanders desires are easily deduced.

122. Uniform and efficient use of the various reconnaissance units is necessary for proper cooperation, and for obtaining a clear picture of the situation.

B. AERIAL RECONNAISSANCE

123. Ability to rapidly cover long distances, to observe terrain which is defiladed to ground observation by the enemy, as well as the possibility of receiving quick personal reports on the situation has made the airplane the most important agent for reconnaissance. But, even when the airplane reports nothing has been seen, one must not always conclude that the enemy is not present.

The airplane is especially useful for strategical reconnaissance missions deep into the enemy's territory.

124. Aerial reconnaissance is executed by observation squadrons that are assigned to all headquarters. These observation squadrons also perform the artillery and infantry airplane missions, as well as transmit information reports. They are divided into reconnaissance and artillery flights.

Definite assignment of missions to be performed and definite assignment of areas to be covered by each, prevents unnecessary expenditure of forces.

125. Observation squadrons attached to general headquarters or army groups perform the most distant reconnaissance and also uniformly patrol long stretches (railroad lines, streams, positions, etc). Army headquarters fully utilize the capabilities of their airplanes, and direct strategical reconnaissance along their own front and on flanks that are unprotected. Corps, when part of an army, perform the tactical reconnaissance in their own front up to 60 kilometers. Close and battle reconnaissance is a duty of the divisions. While on the march, this reconnaissance generally extends one days march beyond the march objective of the division, and during battle, comprises the battlefield of the division. In addition, it is left to the discretion of general headquarters, army groups and corps headquarters to secure for themselves a general picture of the entire situation in their immediate front by sending out airplanes on special missions, (command airplanes).

126. The commander of the troops issues his orders to the commander of the air service squadron or flight. The air service commander designates the airplane teams and is responsible that the fliers have proper orders. Time is always taken for properly issuing orders even during the hottest engagement.

127. As soon as war is declared, aerial reconnaissance of the enemy's railroads, is made. Increase of detraining facilities, construction of depots near railroad stations, and concentration of rolling stock, furnish the first indications of the hostile concentration. When the transportation of troops starts, the entire railroad net is observed day and night. Reports on the railroads used by the enemy, the number, sequence, and rapidity of the daily trains, conditions and location of detraining stations, localities occupied by troops, and the location of hostile airdromes soon give the highest commander a good idea concerning the enemy's concentration.

Aerial photographs, showing daily changes at the same place, are very useful. They at the same time furnish a basis for attacks by the aerial combat units.

128. When observation squadrons once gain contact with the enemy, the next thing is to discover the direction of the hostile advance and the enemy's distribution of forces. This is accomplished by watching roads, villages, and for occupation of airdromes. Discovering lateral movements of hostile troops, by rail or by marching, is important. Aerial photographs, showing the construction of hostile field fortifications, and depots, preparations for crossing a river, extension of the railroad net, and the construction of airdromes are taken as soon as possible. These show the enemy's intentions.

129. During the battle, both in attack and defense, the most important duty of observation squadrons is constant watching of the battlefield.

Sufficient airplanes are attached to the artillery for locating targets and adjusting fire. This permits uninterrupted observation of our own and the hostile battle activities. For this purpose, there are the artillery flights of the observation squadrons, and they are promptly placed under the orders of the artillery commander. Reports on the batteries most actively engaged, on the appearance of new hostile batteries, and on important targets that are not being fired on, form valuable bases for artillery fire orders.

The essential information the highest commander desires to have constantly before him, is probably the conditions in rear of the hostile front- such as arrival of reserves, shifting of troops, concentration of tanks and motor trucks, and the arrival and departure of troops by rail or marching. The commander attempts to gain a clear picture of the general situation along the entire front by sending out special observation planes. He furthermore sends out special infantry planes to reconnoiter the forward movements of our own and the hostile infantry. Troops make themselves known to these special infantry planes by all available means (panels, newspapers, flares, flash lights and visual signals). The infantry plane also reports the fact that our own attack is stopped, the location of hostile strong points that have not yet been thoroughly shaken, hostile command posts, hostile counter attacks, penetrations, and assault troops held in readiness.

130. Accomplishment of aerial reconnaissance missions depends in a high degree on the aerial situation.

Distant reconnaissance is generally carried out by single planes flying at high altitude. This method avoids fighting in the air. When this is not possible, a formation of two or three reconnaissance airplanes generally has sufficient fighting power to solve its reconnaissance tasks in the face of weak hostile pursuit airplanes. Artillery airplanes, which are active for a long time in one and on the same space, frequently require protection against hostile airplanes by other reconnaissance airplanes. In the event of strong hostile aerial activity and when it is desired to force a reconnaissance at a definite hour and over a definite area, then pursuit airplanes escort the reconnaissance airplanes. Monoplace pursuit airplanes are not suited for directly accompanying reconnaissance airplanes.

131. In order to fully utilize the results of aerial reconnaissance, reports are transmitted along the shortest route to the command and to the troops. This is specially true of battle reports. These are of value only when they can immediately be transformed into the action of arms. To accomplish this, the closest cooperation between airplanes and artillery is necessary. The most important information is at once transmitted by wireless to the commander; then the results are written down in clear, concise form, omitting nothing that is important. Important information shown by aerial photography is reported to the commander even before the plates are developed. Personal reports by airplane observers to the commander are valuable.

## C. DISTANT RECONNAISSANCE BY ARMY CAVALRY

132. Strategical reconnaissance is the principal task of the army cavalry.

Prerequisite for its successful execution is tactical superiority in the area to be reconnoitered. Therefore, as a rule, battle with hostile cavalry is sought. Each cavalry detachment down to the patrol attacks hostile cavalry whenever the situation and mission permits. Aggressive reconnaissance serves at the same time for screening purposes and facilitated the service of security.

133. Even after the hostile cavalry has been driven from the field, battle is the best means for further reconnaissance. Advanced hostile detachments are driven back or broken through, in order that our cavalry can push forward to the hostile leading elements and gain an insight into the situation.

134. The area assigned to a cavalry division for reconnaissance does not, as a general rule, exceed 40 to 50 kilometers in width. The depth depends on the location of the reconnaissance objective.

135. Within the area the reconnaissance moves forward, usually organized in patrols, reconnoitering detachments, and main body of the cavalry division. The larger detachments serve as support for the smaller and facilitate the forward movement of the smaller detachments by their greater fighting power. The number and strength of the different reconnoitering detachments are therefore detailed in proper proportion to the strength of the total. Otherwise the reconnaissance lacks sufficient support.

136. Reconnaissance detachments perform the great part of the ground reconnaissance. Their strength varies from a troop to a regiment, according to the probable hostile resistance.

Cyclists, infantry and heavy machine guns on motor trucks, batteries or single guns with caissons, armored cars, tanks, and light wireless stations are attached to them as needed. Occasionally progress can be made only by the assistance of machine guns and field pieces, and having these attached may also deceive the enemy as to our strength.

137. Zones of action corresponding to the available road net are assigned to reconnaissance detachments. The strength of these detachments is governed; by the width of the zones assigned, the information of the enemy, the nature of the terrain, and the mission. The zone of action for a detachment of two troops with attached cyclists, machine guns, and field pieces is rarely more than 15 to 20 kilometers.

Under certain conditions, zones of action are not assigned, and under other conditions, only one side of the zone is designated.

The situation governs the distance between reconnaissance detachments and the main body of the cavalry division. This distance may be several days' march.

138. Instructions are given to each reconnaissance detachment reference its probable route within its zone of action and what lines its patrols will reach daily. Reconnaissance detachments are cautioned against covering too much distance daily. Their hardest work starts when the enemy is encountered.

139. The reconnaissance detachment remains in readiness during the night. Change of nightly location increases security.

140. The reconnaissance detachment is divided, towards the front, into smaller parts, which perform the reconnaissance. The leading "feelers" are the patrols.

The commander of the reconnaissance retains his patrols well in hand. Close objectives, definite missions, and systematic forward movement of patrols from one line to another assure success.

141. Giving patrols distant objectives (distant patrols) is the exception. Such patrols lack support; frequently their reports do not reach the reconnaissance detachment or the cavalry division; and liaison cannot be maintained in territory held by the enemy.

142. The situation and the mission governs the strength of patrols. Patrols are made strong enough to drive hostile patrols off the field and send back reports.

143. According to their importance, patrols are led by efficient officers well mounted, noncommissioned officers and enlisted men having good tactical knowledge and ability to find their way over any country. Personality of the patrol leader assures success.

144. As long as practicable, patrols use existing roads. They advance by rushes from one observation point to another. When contact with the enemy is gained, the roads are abandoned and endeavor is made to gain an insight into conditions in the enemy's line. This if often accomplished on foot, from the flank, by leaving a portion of the patrol behind.

145. The patrols seek well concealed places to pass the night. Touch with the enemy is never lost. Measures for security are taken so that any sudden attack finds the patrol in readiness. Night marches

and frequent changes of position increase security.

146. A consideration of the character of the ground reconnaissance influences the demands made of patrols. Sometimes patrols can only ascertain whether the enemy holds some one point or not, possibly the extent of his position and some points indicating his strength. Patrols can never determine the exact strength of the enemy or the distribution of his forces. Leading elements of hostile columns can be reported, but there is no possibility of reconnoitering between marching hostile columns. Only where a flank is unprotected can a patrol gain a deep insight into hostile conditions.

147. Patrols report to their reconnoitering detachments almost exclusively by one or several mounted messengers. The use of technical means of communication (wire or visual signals) between patrols and reconnaissance detachments is possibly only, when the forward movement of the reconnaissance ceases, and when the reconnaissance assumes more the nature of security.

148. Communication by technical means between reconnaissance detachments and the cavalry division is always attempted. Radio is the best means for this; wire communication is less suitable. If these means are not available, communication is maintained by intermediate stations, relays of runners, or by advanced message centers which are established by the cavalry division.

149. The cavalry division establishes message centers which are used by several reconnaissance detachments in common. They are indispensable when the cavalry division moves in a direction other than the one that is known to its reconnaissance detachments.

150. Only technical means of communication, and principally wireless, are employed by cavalry divisions for communication to the rear. Additional means are wire, automobiles, and airplanes.

151. A small observation squadron is attached to each cavalry division. This squadron is not used for executing distant reconnaissance missions, such as locating the enemy's lines of communication or the hostile concentration. This duty is performed by the observation squadrons attached to general headquarters. The observation squadron attached to the cavalry division assists the division in solving its mission and enables it to gain a deeper view of its zones of action.

152. It is always advisable to attach armored cars to cavalry divisions. These cars are either given independent missions or temporarily attached to support reconnaissance detachments, or they participate in the battle of the cavalry division. They also serve as a means of liaison between reconnaissance detachments and the cavalry division.

153. The importance of reconnaissance detachments decreases with the increasing proximity of the enemy. When there is no longer any room for them in front of the cavalry division and when they no longer have an opportunity to operate on an exposed hostile flank, they rejoin the cavalry division. Their duties are then performed by the close reconnaissance detachments of the brigades and regiments.

D. RECONNAISSANCE BY DIVISIONAL CAVALRY.

154. Close reconnaissance is the principal task of the divisional

cavalry and, divisional cavalry is not relieved from this duty even when a cavalry division is operating in its front. When a cavalry division is not in front, the divisional cavalry is also charged with distant reconnaissance. This duty is performed as by a reconnaissance detachment.

155. The commander of the troops issues the orders for reconnaissance. The method of execution is determined by the cavalry commander. Sending out patrols is generally the business of the cavalry commander. When the commander of the troops himself sends out patrols, he informs the cavalry commander concerning the orders issued to them. The cavalry commander also receives information concerning the close reconnaissance carried on by other arms. Thereby duplication of missions is avoided.

When the cavalry commander has no definite orders, or when he is suddently confronted with an entirely different situation, he conducts the reconnaissance independently and along the lines desired by the commander of the troops.

156. All cavalry commanders are responsible that contact once gained with the enemy is never lost by day or night.

157. The strength of divisional cavalry forces economy in the matter of sending out patrols. The divisional cavalry always maintains a certain fighting strength. It may become necessary to increase the fighting strength of the divisional cavalry by attaching mobile infantry and cyclist detachments, heavy motorized machine gun platoons, field pieces and tanks. Divisional cavalry is always reinforced when it is charged with tactical duties other than close reconnaissance, such as holding crossings, blocking defiles, or when engaged on distant reconnaissance.

158. Orders for close reconnaissance frequently are given from the saddle, and when the reports of the enemy are contradictory. But nevertheless, such orders are thorough and clear so that the commander will obtain the information he desires.

159. The commander of troops must remember that the execution of close reconnaissance missions requires time and that close reconnaissance alone, does not protect his troops against surprise.

In addition to close reconnaissance, every troop unit requires local security.

160. Only in exceptional cases is it possible to perform close reconnaissance and local security by the same patrols. Reconnaissance patrols ride close up to the enemy and are mobile, while the security patrols remain in a fixed position with reference to their own troops. Hence there is a sharp distinction between close reconnaissance patrols and local security patrols.

All arms participate in local security with the division. The divisional cavalry takes over the security in the most important direction, for example, on the march, towards the front; in battle, towards the unprotected flank.

161. In order to receive reports quickly, it is advisable to instruct the patrols to deliver reports at points previously designated.

162. Reconnaissance of the terrain is always associated with close reconnaissance. Besides observing the enemy, the reconnaissance covers; the condition of roads, bridges, passability of the terrain, and the location of good observation stations.

E. BATTLE RECONNAISSANCE BY CAVALRY.

163. Battle reconnaissance by cavalry, may be ordered by the commander of the troops. But even in the absence of such orders, every cavalry commander and subordinate commander is bound to carry on the battle reconnaissance independently. As a rule, each cavalry unit performs battle reconnaissance within its own battle sector, and units that have exposed flanks also reconnoiter on those flanks.

164. Battle reconnaissance consists of continuous observation of the enemy, prior to, during, and after the battle, and serves at the same time as security. It is performed by combat patrols.

165. As far as possible, battle reconnaissance is carried on by mounted men and, when this method is no longer possible, then by dismounted men.

166. Battle reconnaissance is carried on in the front, until the opening of fire. On the flank it is so conducted, that danger is timely perceived and reported to the commander of the troops.

Combat patrols transmit as rapidly as possible information obtained by them to all troops in their vicinity, irrespective of the relation of the patrol to those troops.

F. RECONNAISSANCE BY OTHER ARMS

167. In addition to airplanes and cavalry, all other arms participate to the fullest extent in reconnaissance. The results of their activity completes the picture for attack and defense.

The less amount of cavalry and airplanes attached, the more necessary it is for the other arms to gain information of the enemy by means of patrols and early occupation of suitable points of observation.

Because of their mobility and speed, the cyclist organizations attached to infantry are specially suited for performing reconnaissance missions, and are able to supplement the cavalry reconnaissance and even take its place.

When hostile fire or terrain conditions limit the activity of cavalry, the importance of reconnaissance by infantry patrols is increased.

The infantry prepares for its attack by a reconnaissance screen in which the auxiliary arms participate (light and heavy machine guns, trench mortars, infantry batteries). In order to execute this frontal reconnaissance, battle is not avoided. For this reason light machine guns are frequently attached to reconnaissance units.

When approaching fortified positions, road defiles, strong sectors, rivers, etc., reconnaissance of a technical nature becomes necessary (obstacles, supporting points, routes of approach, places to throw brigades). This is frequently undertaken only at night. But it is started early enough to permit the scouts to gain the desired information of the terrain by daylight. These reconnaissances are executed mainly by engineers ad infantry.

In the artillery, reconnaissance of the enemy and locating observation and firing positions form a material part of the artillery commander's activities. For this purpose, patrols that are generally led by officers (artillery officers patrols) are employed. Occasionally it is advisable to send them ahead with the cavalry. In addition, observation posts and captive balloons, flash and sound ranging units, and triangulation units are used for spotting targets.

Captive balloons are specially valuable for close and battle reconnaissance. A great advantage of this means of observation is the use of telephonic communication between the observer, the commander of the troops, and the artillery down to the firing batteries. It permits direct exchange of views and opinion.

The intelligence troops regularly observe the hostile ground and aerial means of communication. Thus the highest commander gains reliable information concerning the enemy's distribution of forces.

158. Frequently the objective of reconnaissance is gained only by an attack with strong detachments reinforced by artillery.

## G. SECURITY ON THE MARCH.

169. Marching troops secure themselves by reconnaissance, and march formation.

170. The divisional cavalry is employed for the direct security of marching troops. Even when a cavalry division is operating in front, some cavalry is attached to the advance guard. From this is formed a cavalry point which precedes the infantry point. The remainder of the cavalry is employed in direct close reconnaissance. The commander of the main body also has a few troopers available which he uses principally for reconnoitering on the flanks.

Without exception, the commander of the troops retains a small reserve of the divisional cavalry for special purposes, such as, for additional reconnoitering, special security, or for attaching to portions of the main body which leave the march column.

When the commander of the troops assigns divisional cavalry to the commander of the advance guard, the latter issues his orders for reconnaissance and security in accordance with instructions from the commander of the troops.

171. When stronger cavalry is available, special tasks, in addition to reconnaissance and security, are assigned to it. Such tasks may be: temporary occupation of important advanced points along the route of march, occupation of railroad junctions and important buildings, searching larger woods which the troops must traverse, or keeping open defiles and terrain sectors, etc. For this, it is sometimes necessary to attach artillery, infantry and engineers riding in wagons or automobiles, and also to attach machine gun organizations, machine guns on motor trucks and cyclists.

172. The advance guard assures an uninterrupted advance of troops on the march, removes weaker hostile resistance, secures the main body against surprise, and allows it time and space for deployment when the enemy is encountered.

When there is a probability of contact with the enemy, the commander of the troops rides, as a general rule, with the advance guard. This is done in order that timely arrangements for properly conducting the fight can be made and, so that the commander can familiarize himself with the terrain on which the battle will be conducted.

173. Strength and composition of the advance guard depends on the strength of the command, the situation, plans, and the terrain. But, like all detachments, advance guards are limited to the number that is strictly necessary. The strength of the infantry of the advance guard usually varies from one third to one sixth of the total. As a general rule, cyclists, trench mortars, light artillery, light ammunition columns and engineers are attached to an advance guard. It is also advisable to attach light tanks and armored cars, heavy artillery with battery columns, and especially long flat trajectory artillery, signal troops and sanitary troops. It is necessary to attach to an advance guard, a bridge column or portions thereof when the march leads to a river.

Attaching heavy tanks to an advance guard is advantageous especially when it is important to quickly reach and hold a certain sector.

174. As a rule, the commander of an advance guard determines its formation.

Generally he details a vanguard that marches far enough in advance of the main guard to permit the latter an orderly deployment for battle when meeting the enemy. It is frequently advisable to attach a few field pieces to the vanguard.

As a rule, a point company marches 400 to 500 meters in front of the vanguard. This in turn, is preceded by an infantry point which is composed of one officer and one or two infantry squads or machine gun squads and is accompanied by an armored car. The advance guard takes its own measures for flank security.

175. The distance between main body and advance guard is such, that the main body is not immediately drawn into the advance guard action and, that the commander of the troops retains freedom of decision. On the other hand, this distance is such, that the advance guard can be timely supported by the main body. Thus, if the advance guard is weak the distance is less than otherwise. This may also be required by the situation and by difficult terrain.

176. The main body secures its own flanks, especially in close terrain and when the enemy is near. The commander of the main body issues the necessary orders for security by infantry detachments, cyclists or armored cars, which then accompany the marching troops along parallel roads. In this situation, the infantry starts well in advance because the security detachment generally has longer and worse roads than the main column, and may be delayed by searching buildings and woods etc. Good roads are assigned to the armored cars.

In special cases, flank guards are detached ~~either~~ by the main body or by the advance guard.

For determining the strength and composition of flank guards, the degree of danger and the nature of the terrain govern. The necessity of extensive reconnaissance and rapid communication requires cavalry and armored cars to be attached to flank guards. Every flank guard assumes the formation of an advance guard. It either accompanies the advance of the column it is securing, or takes a suitable position to let that column march safely past, and later on rejoins it.

When a march to the front changes into a flank march, it may be of advantage to utilize the advance guard as a flank guard and for the main body to detach a new advance guard.

177. When the situation is not yet clear, it is frequently advisable to send forward machine gun detachments and artillery from the main body to secure the crossing of certain sectors until the advance guard has reached the opposite edge of them.

And in traversing cities, larger villages and extensive woods it may be necessary to arrange for similar security by heavy machine gun detachments and artillery.

This procedure becomes the general rule when contact with the enemy is probable. It is an error on the part of the commander of the troops to expose marching infantry to the enemy without sufficient artillery fire protection.

178. The purpose of a rear guard is to protect a retreating unit against attack. A rear guard never counts on support from the main body. In view of this fact, its strength, composition, and distance from the main body is fixed accordingly.

After disengaging from the enemy on an extensive front, the rear guard is composed of troops from different infantry units. But a regular organization is established as soon as practicable.

As a general rule considerable light artillery is attached to the rear guard, and the rear guard always has cavalry available for reconnaissance. Sufficient machine gun detachments, cyclists and armored cars are also attached. Whether or not engineers are attached, and in what strength, is governed in each case by a consideration of demolitions to be performed.

When troops have been in action, the rear guard makes it possible for the main body to make an orderly retreat. The rear guard may even sacrifice itself to accomplish this.

The rear guard retires from one line of defense to another.

When the enemy no longer forces retreat in battle deployment, the rear guard assumes march formation.

On the march, the rear guard is divided into main guard, rear point and attached cavalry. Its reconnaissance units remain close to the enemy. It depends on conditions, whether or not a cavalry point is needed in addition to a rear point company and infantry point.

179. Anti-aircraft organizations undertake aerial defense along the entire march column in marches to the front, flank, and rear. They move by rushes from position to position, utilizing parallel roads. As long as airplanes threaten the march, they are not incorporated into the march column.

Further means for security against hostile airplanes are: division of the march column into small units, marching alongside the roads, and night marching. Our own pursuit squadrons attack the hostile airplanes.

## H. OUTPOSTS

180. Troops at rest secure themselves by outposts, whose tasks are; to reconnoiter, to protect the resting troops against surprise, to allow them time to deploy for battle, and to prevent the enemy from gaining an insight into conditions within our lines.

181. After considering the diversity of conditions, only general rules can be given in regard to outposts, which must be free of all hard and fast schemes. No more men are detailed for outpost duty than are absolutely necessary to protect the rest of the troops. The kind and strength of outposts depends on the situation and the terrain.

182. When the enemy is distant, it suffices to occupy nearby villages. Greater security is attained by sending single troop units beyond the general resting place. These units in turn secure themselves locally by advanced smaller units. In this, it is specially advantageous, when single units can be advanced to some sector, easy to block or defend.

From this method of security, based on suitable distribution of shelters, to the posting of normal outposts, there are many different methods.

When the enemy is near, outposts formed in sufficient depth, are posted as demanded by the situation and the terrain. But no regular scheme is adopted or adhered to in this matter.

When contact with the enemy is so close that readiness for battle is necessary, then only combat considerations govern the position and formation of outposts. In such a situation, protection is given by troop units placed along a definite line.

When battle is broken off in the evening, but to be continued in the morning, the troops bivouac in their battle positions. In this case, security in front consists of small infantry units, whose pickets, sentries and patrols work as close to the enemy as possible (combat outposts).

In stabilized situations the combat outposts are formed depending on the distance from the enemy. Listening posts watch the obstacles.

183. In every case it is advisable to watch the roads leading towards the enemy. But also, points are occupied from which a view to the front is obtained, and also points which allow the enemy to gain a view into our position and condition. Flanks that are unprotected are secured by refusing the wings or by posting special security detachments.

When it is necessary to consider the unexpected appearance of hostile tanks, proper measures are taken (selection of position in rear of some obstacle, posting single batteries, blocking roads, arranging pits for the tanks to fall into, etc.).

184. When going into rest, the commander of the advance guard or rear guard receives orders reference security. In larger units, these orders contain instructions for reconnaissance, the space to be secured, the location of the main body; and in smaller units they contain instructions for the location of the outpost reserve and must designate whether, in case of hostile attack, the advance guard falls back fighting on the main body or holds its position until arrival of the main body. As a general rule, the main line of resistance is also designated.

185. The commander of the advance guard or the rear guard designates the commander of the outpost and the troops that are to form the outpost. Degree of battle readiness, width of position, and terrain may require several outpost sectors under their own commanders. Important roads and points of the terrain are never selected as outpost limits.

186. The conduct and proximity of the enemy, our own strength, terrain, and ultimate aims govern the strength and composition of outposts.

Artillery is attached to outposts as a general rule, especially when hostile attack is expected. Artillery prepares in day time for action at night, especially range finding. During daylight, cavalry is charged with the security and reconnaissance towards the enemy. At dusk and when the enemy is close, the main body of the cavalry is drawn back.

After a battle, outposts are selected from fresh troops in so far as possible; but on the march, unless otherwise directed, the advance guard or rear guard is charged with securing the main body and furnishing the outposts. In larger commands, outposts are divided into main body and support.

187. The commander of the advance guard, in pursuance to orders from the commander of the troops, directs where outposts will offer the main resistance in connection with adjoining detachments.

When outpost fight merely to gain time, they fall back slowly to that point which the commander of the advance guard has previously designated.

188. The commander of the outpost issues his orders as quickly as possible. The main thing is to execute the most urgent measures as soon as practicable. This principally includes, the occupation of observation points, strong points, and important roads, employment of artillery (observation and barrage, etc), construction of barricades and field fortifications. Based on higher instructions, the outpost commander designates the foremost line of resistance, the distribution of troops along the main line of resistance, the degree of readiness, the kind of shelter, the method of guarding against airplane attacks and the security measures of the outpost reserves.

Strong cavalry is never attached to outpost companies. Reconnaissance is arranged by the outpost commander, in case it is not directed by the commander of the troops or the commander of the advance guard. In view of its weakness, divisional cavalry is employed for reconnaissance and only exceptionally for security.

After personal and local reconnaissance, the outpost commander supplements his primary orders and measures. He is responsible for the posting of all parts of the outpost and he regulates liaison and communication with adjacent units. When in contact with the enemy, special measures for protection against gas attacks are necessary. Gas masks are kept in readiness. Instructions are issued for blockading roads and for constructing pits to entrap hostile tanks and other vehicles.

To facilitate supervision of the outpost service, the commander of the outpost selects his position at some point where reports and messages can be easily sent. His location must be easy to find, and buglers, cyclists, mounted messengers must be on duty there. He also has telephonic connection with the advance guard, main body, outpost reserve, as well as with the outpost companies and artillery.

189. Outposts can be divided into outpost companies, pickets, and sentries and, placed in front of the outpost reserve, which as a general rule is located along the route of march.

190. Occupying an outpost position is made without attracting the enemy's attention. Concealment from aerial observation is necessary.

Reliable communication within the outpost, connecting all portions thereof, is established as soon as possible.

191. As soon as possible, the commanders of all subdivisions of the outpost report in writing to their immediate commander; their location by sketch, and the measures they have taken for security and reconnaissance. They quickly establish and maintain communication with their neighbors. They give orders concerning the rest and the clothing of their troops.

192. The best security consists of uninterrupted close reconnaissance and observation. Favorable points situated in rear of the position are also used for this. All material results of reconnaissance and observation are quickly transmitted to the immediate commander and to adjacent troops.

193. Reliefs are made unobtrusively. Everything which the new commander should know is told him, and the new commander permits departure of the relieved detachment only when he is fully oriented.

194. All detachments in close order secure themselves by stationing sentries at the stacks. The number of sentries varies according to need. These sentries, as well as pickets and other sentries, do not salute.

195. The outposts are always in complete readiness for any attack. Outposts may also sacrifice themselves in order to cover the troops in rear.

## OUTPOST COMPANIES

196. The outpost companies bear the burden of security. Their number and location depends on the general situation.

The commander of the troops orients himself as rapidly as possible as to the terrain, and gives instructions for reconnaissance and security. He determines upon the action to be taken in case of an attack by day or night, gives orders as to the state of readinesss to be maintained (shelter under cover, protection against aerial reconnaissance, whether to erect tents, keeping up fires, or not, gas protection, etc), directs construction of hasty intrenchments and supervises the blockading of roads. Machine guns, light trench mortars, and any field pieces that may be attached are posted principally to command routes of approach.

The outpost companies are designated according to their company numbers. (Outpost company 2./9)

## PICKETS

197. Pickets are posted to protect the outpost companies. Their strength depends on task, importance of location, and proximity of the enemy. Their strength varies from a squad to a platoon.

Pickets act as support for their sentries, and are posted usually at important points in the terrain (bridges, defiles, edges, of villages and woods, crossroads) where a good field of fire obtains, and where they are protected from aerial observation and other hostile observation. It frequently is advisable to attach heavy machine guns to pickets. In special cases they are reinforced by light trench mortars and field pieces. Important pickets are commanded by officers.

Pickets secure themselves by noncommissioned officer's posts, or double sentry posts, and by patrols. In close terrain, it is only necessary to post a few sentries in day time at prominent points. At night a dense chain of sentries is required. But in every case, it is more important to occupy all roads leading from the direction of the enemy, while the intermediate terrain is watched by patrols, than to have a close chain of sentries.

The double sentry posts sent out by pickets, are generally posted not farther from the picket than 500 meters. Noncommissioned officer's posts may be at a greater distance.

The commander of the picket must be easy to find at all times. While inspecting his sentries, he details an assistant to take his place. During the night he remains with his picket.

Pickets are numbered from right to left within the outpost companies.

Sentries of each picket, whether noncommissioned officers or double sentry posts, are numbered in a similar manner.

## INFANTRY SENTRIES

198. Sentries are posted by twos (double sentry posts). When far from the picket, it is desirable to hold the remainder of the squad close to the sentries for relief and suppot at important points. Light machine guns are attached to important sentry posts.

The sentries must have a clear view and must be hidden from the enemy's view, by masking works if necessary. Location at elevated points (trees, houses, steeples, strawstacks, etc) is advantageous for seeing and listening. Sentries are supplied with field glasses. When close to the enemy, it is advisable to change the location of the sentries at night in order to prevent surprise. The two men on post, observe together and must be so close to each other that they can easily communicate.

Instructions are given to the sentries concerning their conduct and whether they can sit or lie down. Sentries, in most cases, intrench themselves. Unless otherwise directed they may smoke. Sentries do not allow anything to distract their attention.

As soon as the sentry observes anything important, a report is made to the commander of the picket. When an attack is uncovered, sentries give the alarm by rapid fire. Sentries inform all patrols passing them of what they have seen.

Sentries allow free passage to all persons known to them. All others are questioned, and in case of doubt, are sent to the picket or some other post designated by the commander. Mounted men, cyclists and people in automobiles halt when challenged; the latter must slacken speed in time. Any one disobeying the orders of a sentry is shot down.

At night, every one approaching is challenged by "Halt-who goes there". The piece is brought to the ready. If the challenged party does not halt at the third call he is shot down.

Individual officers of the enemy with a few men accompanying, who make themselves known as authorized messengers, and also deserters arriving, are not treated as enemies. They are disarmed and sent to the picket, and from there, to the outpost company- the officers with eyes blindfolded.

All sentries receive special orders, which cover:- Information of the enemy and villages around, portions of the terrain to be specially watched (visible stretches of roads, defiles, bridges which the enemy must cross in his approach), location of our advanced detachment, designation of his own sentry post, conduct in case of hostile attack, location and designation of neighboring posts, whether to take up communication therewith, location of the picket, of the company, roads leading thereto, and similar directions.

When possible, all sentries are supplied with a sketch of the foreground containing the name of villages, etc.

Relief within a noncommissioned officers post is regulated by the respective noncommissioned officer; in case of double sentry posts, by the commander of the picket. The commander of the relief convinces himself that the new sentries know their orders, that the old sentries turn the orders over properly, and that the new sentries thoroughly understand them.

## INFANTRY PATROLS

199. Whether cavalry is out in front or not, close reconnaissance is carried on by infantry patrols.

The number and strength of patrols sent out towards the enemy, their equipment with machine guns, as well as instructions for probable readiness for gas attacks, depend on the general situation and mission. Selection of patrol leaders is very important: the leaders themselves select the most suitable men to accompany them.

Officers and specially efficient noncommissioned officers are selected for important reconnaissance missions. It may be necessary to send forward a regular chain of patrols for mutual protection and prevention of capture.

Cunning and efficiency, keen sight and decisive action; audacity and intrepidity is demanded of every patrol. Every patrol thoroughly studies the terrain in order to give information thereof and to serve as guide in case of need.

Time of return and roads to be taken are indicated in orders. This permits maintenance of a regular patrol service by timely sending out other patrols.

At night and for the purpose of increased security, it sometimes is necessary to send squads beyond the line of sentries to suitable points in the terrain, to remain there either until relieved, or for a definite time.

When crossing the line of sentries, patrols, inform the nearest sentries about their task and when returning inform the sentries of the results accomplished.

Patrols inside of the line of sentries, watch the intermediate terrain which is not held by sentries, and serve as a means of liaison between sentries and adjacent detachments. Their number and strength differs according to the space between sentries, and depends on the terrain and proximity of the enemy.

## J. SCREENING

200. Screening towards the enemy in the air and on the ground is necessary on the flank as well as in front and is accomplished offensively or defensively. Screening is principally performed by airplanes and by cavalry. But all other reconnaissance and security detachments perform their share of screening.

201. The main task of airplanes is to prevent hostile aerial reconnaissance behind our screening line. They support the offensive screening on the ground by aerial activity and aerial attacks. In defensive screening on the ground, and when there is little hostile aerial activity, our aerial forces are held back if weak. Hostile aerial reconnaissance in force is met by a concentrated aerial attack

and employment of anti-aircraft guns.

202. Offensive screening on the ground is performed best by defeating the hostile cavalry. Hostile reconnaissance activity along roads not used by our columns is stopped by sending out strong detachments, frequently reinforced by field pieces, heavy machine guns, and tanks.

Defensive screening is best in a sector that can be crossed only at definite points. Crossings and roads are blockaded and defended. Here machine guns are specially valuable. In case of need, artillery (even only single field pieces), and trench mortars are attached to the different defensive groups.

Strong detachments are posted in readiness near important places that will probably be pierced by the enemy.

During defensive screening, reconnaissance activity is continuous. Reconnaissance detachments with cyclists and machine guns are sent out to restrict the hostile communication and liaison service.

203. In each kind of screening, cover against aerial observation is necessary and that is best accomplished, by keeping off the roads and away from villages in day time, and by avoiding light and fire at night.

--oOo-----

# IV MARCHES

## A. GENERAL PRINCIPLES.

204. Open warfare demands quick execution of all decisions, and demands fresh troops for the battle. Arrangements for marches are made to meet both these requirements. The highest commander decides upon the length of marches necessary, and whether consideration can be given to save the troops. Excessive demands not only weaken the fighting power but also the morale of the troops. Railroads, motor trucks, and other vehicles can be employed to transport the troops and their baggage.

The road net, which is reconnoitered under certain conditions, governs the assignment of units to different roads. Maps do not always give correct information.

Marching in broad deployment saves the troops and places them in readiness for battle; while the formation and the march of long columns, as well as deployment from columns requires time and uses up forces. On the other hand, a unit marching against the enemy is better held in hand by the leader when united in one column.

In larger commands, the division generally marches as a unit on one road.

205. When larger troop units make several day's marches without hostile interference, a march table is drawn up governing the marches. This table contains, in addition to assignment of roads, the march objectives to be reached daily, and the localities for bivouacs. Corps headquarters and division headquarters are designated early, so that the system of communications can be completed as early as possible. This gives the entire movement a firm foundation.

## B. MARCHING

206. All orders for a march depend principally on whether or not contact with the enemy is probable. If contact is not expected, the troops receive consideration (ordinary marches). In that case, the march is made in smaller units and by arms. The subsistence and baggage trains remain with the troops.

When contact with the enemy is probable (campaign marches), considerations of readiness for battle take the foreground. This requires organization of the troops into mixed tactical units and measures for security. Orders as to the manner of carrying gas masks may be necessary. Subsistence and baggage trains follow in close order.

207. All troops march in route column, the cavalry by twos, cyclists by twos, or in single file. When road conditions are specially favorable, the march depths may be shortened by broader formation.

Movements of units carried in motor trucks are regulated by special orders. These units are incorporated in the march column only exceptionally, because they cannot maintain the rate of march of

/lkb

the infantry for any length of time. They are either assigned to separate roads or follow by rushes. But the closer contact with the enemy becomes, the more assurance there must be that they will be on hand when required.

Tanks are unsuited for long marches. When the forward movement exceeds 12 kilometers, special transport means are necessary, such as railroads, motor trucks and trailers.

Aerial units avoid changing flying fields every day. They are moved in longer rushes (several days' march).

208. Strict discipline on the march is necessary. It saves the power of the troops. The subordinate commanders, company commanders, troops, battery, and column commanders are not bound to fixed places. They ride wherever they can best supervise the movement of their men. One officer marches at the rear of each unit. Individual changes in the wearing of the uniform are forbidden; necessary changes, such as opening collars, are timely ordered.

As soon as the command "route step" is given, the men may converse, sing, and smoke, and carry the rifle as desired on right or left shoulder, or suspended. Courtesies are not rendered without direct orders therefor. Superiors, causing the column to march past them, are freely looked at.

209. The march column marches as a unit on the part of the road that suits it best. In mixed commands, the infantry has the preference of the best part of the road.

In exceptional cases, the column divides and marches along both sides of the road. Vehicles remain on that part of the road that suits them best and march as a unit. Units with few vehicles thereby protect themselves against hostile aerial reconnaissance when the sides of the road are lined with trees.

In every case, a portion of the road is kept open for the use of cavalry, cyclists and automobiles. When a unit is moved up in front of another, orders are issued to pass a certain side of the column, so as to avoid crossing. When roads are narrow, proper space is secured by closing up on one side of the road. Unnecessary and fast driving past a column on the part of automobiles and cycles shows disregard for the comfort of the troops and is forbidden.

To prevent the march column from elongating, care is taken that the proper alignments and distances are kept between ranks, and files, and vehicles.

In difficult conditions, connecting files who are usually officers, mounted, or in automobiles, see that different units in the column maintain proper distance from the unit in its front; the leading elements of the main body especially, never lose connection with the rear elements of the advance guard.

When marching in several columns, airplanes can quickly inform the commander of the troops in regard to march objectives reached and special events with the differenc columns. In open terrain, instructions are given, that the leading elements of the columns make themselves known to the airplanes by displaying large

/lkb

signal cloths. Construction of telephone lines between the different columns on the march takes much time and considerable personnel, and is resorted to only in exceptional cases; wireless communication suffices in most cases. Wireless is not used as long as it is necessary to hide the march from the enemy.

If units are withdrawn from the march column, orders are at once issued to the leader of the succeeding unit, so that it can close up and take the right road.

210. Adherence to a march rate is the principal requirement for the smooth execution of any march. It best prevents delays.

The rate of march of troops with pack animals is less than that of other troops. It cannot be increased for long distances, as the pack animals are soon exhausted.

When roads are bad or covered with snow, the leading detachment is changed from time to time. In strong wind, the troops marching on the exposed side of the road, are frequently changed.

211. To offset minor changes in the march depths, distances are maintained between units. Between companies and troops the distance is ten paces; between battalions, cyclist companies, machine gun companies, trench mortar companies, batteries and train columns, fifteen paces; between infantry regiments or artillery battalions forty paces; between divisions, one hundred and twenty paces.

Mounted officers, led horses, etc are counted into the column depth, and are not considered in the distances.

Increase of these distances is undesirable, any distance lost is made up by gradually increasing the pace.

212. At the beginning of the march, the commander of the troops makes certain that the troops march as ordered. Shortly after the start of the march, he directs a short half for adjustment of uniform, equipments, for tightening cinchas, and for relief. Other halts are arranged according to the length of the march, weather and nature of the terrain. Like the necessary rests for meals during long marches, these halts are published to the troops in the orders for the march, so that officers may ride ahead and make arrangements, and so that the troops will get the greatest benefit from them. Reference halts for meals, locations are selected near water. Halts are best made by groups, shortening the march depths, and near villages situated on or near the route of march. In forming groups, differences in the march are offset prior to the halt. Considerations of cover against aerial observation govern the assembly formations taken by the troops.

213. Great heat demands special precautionary measures. The most effective are: frequent and regulated drinking; and carrying coffee and tea is advisable. It may also be advisable to increase the distances between the different units and to interrupt the march during the hottest hours of the day.

During extreme cold, increased rations heighten the resisting power of men and animals.

/lkb

Stimulants (alcohol) on the march are forbidden. The dangers of drinking alcohol on the march are expressly explained.

214. Carrying the knapsacks on wagons materially increases the marching capacity of troops, but, because of the necessity of a great numerical increase of vehicles, this is done only in exceptional cases. On the other hand, company vehicles can be used to carry the knapsacks of the sick and disabled and even for carrying such men.

215. Forced marches always interfere with subsequent marches, or requirements. But they may be necessary when the main point is to participate in a decisive battle. In such a case, halts for rest are confined to those absolutely necessary. The march achievements can be temporarily increased by divulging to the men the object of the march, by giving frequent rests, by more frequent and better subsistence, and by caring more for the comfort of the men.

216. In the zone of active operations, night marches are frequently made for protection against hostile aerial reconnaissance and to surprise the enemy. But night marches fatigue the troops materially and hence are kept up only for a short time.

When hostile airplanes approach at night, protection is secured by abandoning the middle of the road, halting and lying down until the parachute flares from the airplanes are burned out.

In night marches, special attention is given to road reconnaissance and to connection between the different units by means of mounted messengers, cyclists and connecting files. Numerous short halts timed by watch are made; these are preferred to fewer and longer halts, as the latter make the troops sleepy.

Guide posts and signs are erected for stragglers, mounted messengers, and subsistence vehicles.

217. In crossing pontoon bridges, the orders issued by the engineer officers of the bridge trainsare strictly obeyed.

Infantry crosses in march column, without cadence; cavalry crosses dismounted and in single file or by twos; in the latter case both troopers on the outside of their horses. After crossing troopers remain at the walk, so that the horses still crossing do not become restless.

Wheeled units cross in single column. The drivers remain mounted or on the wagon seat, and keep to the center of the bridge. The accompanying men march on both sides of the animals; brakes remain guarded. Motorized artillery, tanks, automobiles, and other very heavy vehicles cross field bridges only with large distances between vehicles and very slowly; under certain conditions, they cross only on heavy field bridges.

Halts are not made immediately before or after crossing; the entrances of the bridge are kept free for following units.

Marching across railroad bridges requires special and time-consuming preparations in case of animals and vehicles, such as placing flooring.

/lkb

If the road is under traffic, permission to cross is secured from the military railroad authorities prior to crossing.

218. When streams that are not bridged must be crossed, the troops use ferries. The horses stand on ferries heads upstream. Restless horses are either placed in the center or are temporarily left behind. Vehicles are secured by locking brakes or placing blocks under wheels. Points of debarkation are immediately cleared.

As a rule infantry and cavalry are crossed in pontoons. Horses swim alongside and draw the pontoon to the opposite bank. The commanders decide whether infantry shall remove packs prior to entering pontoons, whether packs are to be left behind, or taken along. Commanders must remember the disadvantages of leaving packs behind, as bringing them up subsequently is very difficult when crossing a river. If the men keep the packs on their persons, they sit down with their backs against the sides of the pontoon.

## C. MARCH ORDERS.

219. Troops are assembled by march orders and formed so that a smooth march is assured and that surprise by the enemy is prevented.

220. The troops are timely informed by warning orders that march orders are about to be issued, and when possible, these warning orders state the time of starting, the first objective, and the probable duration of the march. Then the troops can make proper preparation.

221. Prior to the start, the route of march is reconnoitered, when it is not in our undisputed possession, and when there is a possibility that the enemy or inhabitants may cause delay by blockades or destruction of bridges. In case the reconnaissance is not made by the outposts, it is the task of the cavalry airplanes, or specially selected officers sent ahead, either mounted ot in automobiles or armored cars. The results of this reconnaissance may necessitate special measures for example; attaching engineers, road construction and labor units with special tools, and bridge trains to the advance guard, arranging the halts to conform to the times for repair work, etc.

222. The basis for march orders is the exact calculation of distance and time. Consideration is given tothe roads from and to bivouacs of the different units.

In long marches, large troop units under favorable conditions require on the average of 15 minutes per kilometer if the terrain is flat or slightly hilly. This includes short rests.

Mounted units and motorized formations march more rapidly, and small infantry units marching along also can cover more ground, particularly for shorter stretches.

When roads are good, the rate of march at night is the same as in daytime; but it decreases when roads are bad and when it is very dark.

The same holds good in hilly country and mountains.

/lkb

The hour of starting depends on the situation, weather, season, and length of the march. An early start and leaving the old bivouac while still dark is better than arriving in the new bivouac after dark. In the case of mounted troops, their rest ceases under usual conditions about two hours prior to starting, and it does not begin after finishing the march as soon as for the dismounted troops. Overhasty feeding early in the morning diminishes the strength and efficiency of the animals.

Method of assembly is governed by strength of command, extension of bivouacs, and tactical considerations.

The march column is formed under protection of the outposts, which do not join the march column until portions of the advance guard (or rear guard) cross the outpost line.

As a general rule, all troop units are assembled in the march direction.

To assemble large masses at some one point prior to commencing the march is seldom advisable because of the danger of hostile aerial reconnaissance and other reasons.

When several troop units start from the same point, their arrival at that point is so regulated that no unit is forced to wait any length of time.

Unnecessary detours are prohibited. A start for the assembly place is never made earlier than absolutely necessary.

It is generally preferable to form the march column by having the separate units join the column, depending on their bivouac locations, at points along the route of march that offer protection from hostile aerial observation.

Anti-air-craft organizations are assigned to the different groups.

223. The sequence of troops in the march column is so arranged that they are at the proper place for their probable employment in battle, and so that they can rapidly deploy. Units are kept intact as much as possible. Correct arrangement of the march column is one of the first steps towards gaining the victory.

The march sequence of the security detachments (advance guard, etc) is generally regulated by their commander; however, for simplifying orders, the commander of the troops may regulate that matter in his orders.

The commander of the troops designates the order of march for the main body. He designates a commander of the main body to whom the commanders of the different units report as they join the march column; and thereby they and their troops become part and portion of the column.

The commander of the main body supervises the timely starting of the different units of the main body and their cohesion during the march. He arranges for continuous liaison with the advance guard (rear guard) and flank guards if any, and takes measures for necessary flank protection and protection against aircraft. His duties as commander of the main body cease without further orders, when the commander of the troops issues orders for deployment.

/lkb

224. When advancing to the front, one infantry unit, the engineers, and one signal corps unit march as a general rule at the head of the main body.

The mass of the artillery marches as far forward in the main body as is permissible with security and dependent on its probable employment in battle. Infantry batteries and any other artillery that may temporarily be under orders of the infantry, marches in the column with its infantry units. If the artillery columns are long and if danger threatens from aircraft, or in close terrain, infantry units are inserted in the artillery column. The remainder of the infantry marches in rear of the artillery; the sanitary company, the light ammunition columns, the battery columns, and all other units attached to the division.

When the bridge train is not attached to the advance guard, it marches at the end of the main body. The bridge train attached to corps marches either at the end of the main body or with the field trains.

Portions of the signal corps units, that are employed during the march for establishing communications, have full freedom of movement along and in the march column.

In the retreat, the order of march is reversed.

225. The system of communications extends forward with the march. The signal corps staff officer and the signal corps officers with troops make timely arrangements for this. Construction and laying of the telephone line is begun as far as the situation permits, even before the start of the march.

Construction in the march column is generally carried on between advance guard and main body in such a way, that the construction squads constructing certain portions overtake the squads in front and pass them. Regular relief is arranged. Telephone stations are established at the end of each construction sector. These stations are made known to the troops in the march orders and facilitate the transmission of order, reports, and messages during the march from rear to front and flank. When telephone lines are no longer required, they are taken down by units in rear. Two wireless stations are employed for communication with higher headquarters in rear. One of these stations works while the other marches.

Corresponding measures are taken in the retreat.

226. The combat train, which is formed by battalion or section, marches with the troops; that of the infantry batteries marches with the infantry to which batteries are attached. The combat train of the security detachments closest to the enemy marches with the main body of each security detachment.

Field trains, assembled by division, generally march separately. The different units of field trains are usually assembled only after the troops have started. The different units are then brought to the point of assembly for the entire train. As a general rule, the subsistence sections of the field trains follow at a definite distance either in rear of the main body or in rear of the combat train, while the baggage sections follow at a greater distance.

/lkb

When the situation is not yet clear and when the troops enter battle, it is best to have field trains march to definitely designated points and there await further orders.

In the retreat the field trains are sent on ahead; in a flank march they march on the side that is not threatened by the enemy.

The field train of a cavalry division operating far in front requires special attention and orders. In its movements, following up the cavalry division, it must not interfere with the following-up troops.

227. In large units, considerations of subsistence may require single subsistence sections to be inserted in the march column of the combat troops. When a battle is imminent, ammunition supply and need of field hospitals receive the first consideration. Then, the combat section is formed from ammunition columns, field hospitals and any available engineer subsistence column; this combat section marches in rear of the subsistence section, or directly in rear of the fighting troops; on the retreat it marches ahead of the main body without distance.

/lkb

## V. SHELTER AND BIVOUACS

### A. GENERAL PRINCIPLES

228. It is the duty of all commanders to endeavor to provide good shelter for their troops. Good shelter conserves the fighting power of troops. Troops appreciate the efforts of the commanders along this line.

We distinguish between billets, village bivouac and bivouac. The first is always preferred. No matter how scant and crowded, it provides better rest than camping in the open. Therefore, all possibilities of shelter are utilized to the fullest extent. Only in the absence of villages, or when tactical considerations make it necessary, especially if the enemy is near, do troops go into bivouac. Troop units, partially sheltered in billets and partially in bivouac, are designated to be in village bivouac.

In all cases, the commander of the troops takes steps for the anti-air-craft defense.

The best protection against airplane reconnaissance and aerial attack is correct utilization of the terrain, using available cover, and seeking cover at the first alarm (aerial alarm sentries).

Field pieces, vehicles, and automobiles are never posted regularly, as regular positions indicate too much to aircraft. When they cannot be posted, under trees, hedges, etc. they should be well camouflaged.

229. Prior to a practice march, the commander of the troops issues his orders for going into bivouac as early as practicable and also states the method of their security. Retrograde marches for going into bivouac are avoided. The commander of the troops issues orders for going into bivouac to all units down to the battalion. In this way issuance of orders is facilitated, and the commander of the troops, knowing where the billets are, can issue his orders earlier for the following day. Subordinate commanders shift their troops to offset inequalities, but report the fact at once to the next higher commander.

231. Supplementary orders for shelter are avoided. They interfere with the rest of the troops and damage the reputation of the commander. When conditions are not yet cleared up, a halt should first be made along the route of march, meals supplies from field kitchens, until orders can be issued for taking up shelter.

### B. BILLETS AND VILLAGE BIVOUAC.

232. When contact with the enemy is unlikely, considerations are first given to comfort of the troops, good shelter and good subsistence. The spaces to be occupied depend on the number and size of the available villages, their location in relation to the route of march, the depth of march columns, the distance covered and to be covered the next day, and the time of resuming the march. It is generally simplest and most comfortable for the troops, when the entire space of shelter is about the same in length as the march column.

/lkb

The different troop units are assigned to villages according to the order of march or in accordance with the order of march intended for the next day. By mixing the arms, all shelter and stables are best utilized. Anti-air-craft units are equally distributed among the villages.

In so far as special considerations do not demand otherwise, the villages nearest the route of march are more densely garrisoned.

Field trains are brought up to their troops.

Shelter for aerial units depends on the availability of a suitable level field.

233. When the enemy is close, tactical considerations take priority. Men are quartered more densely. Strong infantry detachments with machine guns and batteries are quartered in the villages nearest the enemy. Artillery is never quartered by itself. Reference the air service, the pursuit squadrons are well forward; attack squadrons behind them, observation squadrons near their headquarters; and bombing squadrons farther in rear. Replacement columns are farthest from the enemy. In a threatening situation, field trains are not brought up to the troops.

Villages or other localities with good road and wire communication are selected for all headquarters. It should be remembered that prominent points are specially exposed to bombardment attacks and that they greatly interfere with staff work.

234. Commanders are assigned to groups (going into shelter) that are formed according to the order of march. They conduct the troops to the designated localities and report the distribution of these troops to the commander of the troops. Otherwise troops remain under the orders of their regular commanders.

Billets are prepared in advance in so far as conditions permit and in cooperation with the civil authorities as far as possible. Even when the distribution of troops is ordered during the march, it is well to send quartermasters ahead. This enables the troops to go into rest quicker than if they arrive unannounced.

For rapidly sheltering the troops, especially in enemy country, a shortened procedure is frequently necessary. In that case the entire troop units are assigned to certain sections of the village, headquarters and smaller detachments to definite streets and houses. The distribution is made by officers sent ahead; in larger localities it is best to have the town major, who is designated to take charge of billeting, ride ahead, accompanied by an officer from each troop unit. In making the distribution, consideration is given to the tactical conditions, hence mounted troops are generally sheltered farthest away from the enemy.

Information is always obtained, either in cooperation with the civil authorities or by questioning inhabitants, whether or not epidemics are prevalent in the locality. Infected houses and stables are not occupied and are plainly marked.

/lkh

235. In each locality, the senior officer assumes the duties of town major, without further orders, unless higher headquarters specially designate this officer. Officers from the regimental commander up are authorized to designate some other officer for this duty.

The town major supervises the degree of battle readiness, takes the necessary security measures and makes arrangements for defense against aircraft. He arranges for maintenance of the administrative work and for construction of the necessary telephone lines.

If the village has been taken after a fight, sufficient forces are placed at the disposition of the town major to search the place for stragglers of the enemy, to gather in all arms, to confiscate and salvage all supplies.

236. In large villages the town major is assisted by an officer. This assistant is the commander of all guards and regulates the details of his guards according to the directions of the town major. In addition, a sanitary officer and an officer of the day is attached to the staff of the town major when required. All officers and non-commissioned officers are under the orders of the assistant to the town major. These care for the administration and discipline within their commands and supervise the execution of all measures taken by the town major.

237. Exterior guards may become necessary for securing the village and preventing traffic on the part of the inhabitants with the outside. These exterior guards occupy the exits, barricades, and important points on the edge of the village and foreground., so that it will be impossible to surprise resting troops. When necessary, machine guns, light trench mortars or field pieces are attached to exterior guards.

238. The police service within the villages is carried on by interior guards. Their strength depends on the number of sentries necessary, and it is always confined to the lowest requirements . Sentries in the interior service of troop units are not a part of the interior guards proper. In smaller commands, the exterior guards may also perform the duties of interior guards.

Railroads and their buildings are secured according to the demands of the military railroad authorities. These officials maintain order at the railroad stations; railroad guards being under their orders for that purpose.

239. The general principles for outposts hold good for all village guards as well as for the sentries in the interior service of troop units, except that all village guards salute.

One musician is detailed to each guard.

240. The quarters and telephone office of the town major and his assistant are situated on the main street and are plainly marked. In the telephone officer is displayed a sketch of the lines of communications and a list of headquarters and troops quartered in that village or locality. Every troop unit that arrives, immediately establishes connection with this telephone office and reports to the town major.

/lkb

The offices of the headquarters are marked in daytime by flags or guidons, at night by screened lanterns. The shelters of troops and sanitary establishments are marked, but names and numbers of units are not given. Cellars offering security against bombardment attacks are plainly marked.

241. When the locality is crowded, it may be necessary for the town major to take special measures to maintain order, especially after dark. This includes; the posting of strong interior guards, early closing of saloons; prohibition of sale of alcoholic liquors, ordering lights out early, timely assignment of the different wells and pumps, and regulation of vehicle traffic.

242. Strict road discipline, order, and cleanliness is demanded, as well as obedience to all sanitary measures laid down by the sanitary service. Proper arrangements are made for latrines, etc. It is important to examine all wells and pumps and to mark those that are found to be impure. Wells, used for drinking water only, are marked. Where there is doubt as to purity of water, placards are attached to all wells and pumps under suspicion, cautioning the users to boil the water prior to use. In all such cases, it is advisable to issue weak tea for drinking purposes.

When the troops remain for a long time in a locality, all arrangements tending towards the health and comfort of the troops are extended. In this matter, the skill and the energy of the town major, the sanitary, veterinary, officers and supply officers find a large field of activity.

243. Doubtful conduct on the part of the populace requires special security measures such as, taking hostages, keeping houses open, stopping automobile traffic on the part of inhabitants, stopping all except military telephone communication, and threatening the inhabitants with punishment for violation of orders. Strong interior guards, alert sentries, and alarm readiness prevent surprise.

Harsh treatment of a quiet populace is not only useless but absolutely injurious to our own interests. However, it is always well to keep distance. Wanton destruction of houses and private property and wasting supplies are sharply punished. Any attempt at looting is suppressed by inflicting harsh punchiment.

244. Proximity of the enemy demands alarm readiness. Each man keeps his arms and equipment ready so that he can fall in at a moments notice. Defense of the locality from one line to another is prearranged.

Consideration of animals demands special measures. To avoid locking them in yards and stables, all yards should be connected by gaps in fences or fences razed. Troops rest fully dressed and equipped near their animals. Officers are with their troops. Sentries are posted outside the yards and stables. It may also be necessary to hold the horses bridled and saddled during the night and outside the stables in the yards, on the village square, or even outside the village. When the situation is precarious, all vehicles remain hitched up.

/lkb

245. For rapid alarm, the "general" is sounded. The orders therefore are given by the senior officer or by the town major. At the sudden appearance of the enemy, any officer or officer's aspirant may give orders to sound the "general". All other signals other than the "general", "aerial alarm" and "gas alarm" are forbidden. The "general" and "aerial alarm" are taken up immediately by all musicians within the locality, the "gas alarm" only when it is still possible.

The night alarms easily cause confusion among resting troops. Therefore, everyone ordering an alarm to be sounded must seriously consider whether it is not possible to rouse the troops in some other way, for example, by telephone. The troops are drilled in immediate assembly without signal (still alarm).

246. In case of alarm, the commander of the troops gives orders reference the degree of battle readiness and places for assembly, if he desires to assemble troops sheltered in different localities. Streets and roads are designated for assembly places at night.

The town major designates an assembly place for each troop unit and the roads leading thereto.

The place of assembly is selected so that troops can quickly assemble and reach the points they have to occupy without interference with other troops. Streets within the village are avoided as much as possible, and when they are used, one half of the street is left free for other traffic. The place of assembly for artillery, machine guns, trains and motorized organizations is at their parks.

At the "alarm" signal, troops assemble at their places of alarm or occupy points assigned them. The conduct of mounted troops and trains is prescribed in orders by the town major; the same is true in case of gas and aerial attack alarms. The guards regulate their conduct in accordance with orders issued by the town major. When the enemy enters the locality by surprise, each individual defends himself.

247. When troops have insufficient room in the localities assigned them, the remainder bivouac in the vicinity of buildings, on squares, in streets, yards, gardens and outside the village (village bivouac).

Regulations covering billets govern the portions under roof, regulations covering bivouacs govern those in bivouac.

## C. B I V O U A C

248. Because of hostile aerial reconnaissance, bivouacs are by small groups and irregular. Cover of terrain, subsistence, available wood and water, etc., as well as the special requirements of the different arms govern the grouping of the single bivouacs. Care is taken to protect the artillery.

False bivouacs and false works may mislead the hostile aerial reconnaissance and divert airplane attacks. Measures for protection against artillery fire and aerial attacks are important (construction of masked covered trenches).

/lkb

249. Bivouacs in woods (only during foliage) are specially favorable. Measures are taken against danger from fires. In open terrain, the different bivouacs are well separated and use is made of woods, dams, defiles, gardens, hop-fields, and corn-fields. Field pieces and vehicles are irregularly placed and well camouflaged. Existing shade is fully utilized. Good liaison is valuable. In making trails, care must be taken, lest trails leading into an otherwise well hidden bivouac betray to the airplane the presence of troops. Vehicles are well concealed or dispersed over the terrain.

250. The place of bivouac should have a dry sub-soil and offer as much cover against wind and weather as possible. In this respect, woods are preferred. Meadows are almost always unsuitable. Proximity of swamps and sloughs is undesirable because of mosquitoes, and under certain conditions endanger health.

251. Each unit arriving at the place of bivouac immediately arranges itself there. Subsequent shifting about interferes with rest and is warranted only in exceptional cases.

Higher headquarters are sheltered in nearby villages or houses so as to facilitate office work.

252. In every bivouac, the senior officer is the bivouac commander without special orders therefor. He rides ahead of his troops to locate suitable places and takes his own bivouac at some easily found place. In other respects, his duties correspond to those of a town major. He is particularly responsible that all available auxiliary means that may be found or offer themselves are fully and systematically utilized (bringing in straw, wood, etc) so that troops will have rest and protection against the elements. Whether or not fires may be lighted, depends on the general situation; in most cases this is not permitted nor possible.

As in the case of village bivouac, the bivouac commander has assistants: - an assistant bivouac commander, a sanitry officer, an officer of the day, etc.

In bivouacs, sanitary measures receive especial attention. Prior to leaving the bivouac, garbage and residues of the slaughter houses are thrown into pits and covered with at least three feet of earth; the same is true for latrines. In summer, every time a latrine is used, the contents thereof are covered with a thin layer of earth for protection against flies.

253. A bivouac is secured in the same manner as billets or village bivouac. The place of the bivouac is generally the place of assembly in case of alarm.

When the entire unit is divided into many groups, many detailed instructions are necessary for conduct in case of alarm.

254. When the general situation permits, the bivouac commander requires the musicians to play at stated hours, and also play retreat.

The different troops units fall in for roll call and conduct evening prayer, after which all retire.

The signals for alarm in billets and village bivouac are used in bivouac.

/lkb

## VI. MEETING ENGAGEMENT AND METHOD OF ATTACK

### INTRODUCTORY STAGES OF THE FIGHT.

255. Uncertainty and lack of clearness of the situation are the rule in open warfare. When aerial reconnaissance is absent, the opponents principally gain knowledge of each other through actual contact. Thus, the meeting engagement generally consists of deployment from march columns.

256. The course of the engagement between the leading security detachments, is of special importance to the general course of the battle. This charges the commander of the whole, who is with the leading detachment, with a peculiar responsibility. He cannot make his decision dependent on further time-consuming reconnaissance. He issues orders frequently when uncertain and assumes that the enemy also is unprepared for battle.

Hostile fire, striking a march column by surprise, should not immediately stop the march to the front, but should cause the troops to push forward.

257. Vigorous attack is always advisable. Knowledge of the general plan and knowledge of the general situation, good observation and good terrain conditions afford the proper basis for this action.

By selecting his position sufficiently close to the front, the commander of the troops keeps the course of action in his hands.

258. That side which is better prepared, will have all the advantages in entering battle. Attempt is made to lay down the law to the enemy in the very beginning, in order to secure for ourselves freedom of action. The proper means therefor are: early starting of the main body in the direction where the decision is sought, and timely deployment.

259. By placing the units alongside of each other, we obtain lateral deployment. This leads the units to fight individually from depth and avoids mixing the different units.

260. A broad reconnaissance, a protective screen of cavalry, and advance and flank guards must prevent the enemy from making ground observation; his aerial reconnaissance must be hindered by the air service and by quickly preparing means of defense.

261. On the other hand, the enemy also will endeavor to increase our difficulties of gaining an insight into his conditions, by a broad extension of weak advanced detachments, to which artillery may be attached. It is therefore necessary to quickly drive off these advanced troops with leading security detachments, in order to prevent our forward movement from being delayed and to avoid making unnecessary marches with our troops.

Only actual battle brings complete clearness of the measures and intentions of the enemy. The battle forces the enemy's hand and forces him to show his forces. Artillery and light trench mortars, attached to the leading security detachments, draws the hostile artillery fire and breaks down unforeseen resistance.

/en

262. The advance guard has the special duty of gaining sufficient time and room for deployment of the main body and of securing good observation for the mass of the artillery. It is frequently best to quickly deploy portions of the advance guard artillery along a broad front, thereby compelling the enemy to make detours and to advance cautiously. This is the case especially when the enemy has gained an advantage in deployment for battle, or appears to have gained it. A further duty of the advance guard artillery is to support the advance guard infantry in the capture of important points in the terrain in front and on flank; commanding heights, favorable observation points for artillery, villages, and woods.

263. In most cases, the advance guard takes up a broader extension than is indicated by its strength for the execution of a decisive battle. But the main body soon relieves it. And the enemy at first is uncertain as to the strength of the advance guard. Employing the advance guard artillery in groups will materially deceive the enemy.

264. When it is certain that the enemy has the advantage in readiness for battle, then caution is necessary. In order to avoid envelopment in the beginning, and to avoid fighting against a superiority in numbers continually, the commander of the troops evades a decisive battle until sufficient forces have arrived and until sufficient time is gained for employing the artillery.

It may even be advisable to withdraw the entire advance guard or a part of it, to save it from costly fighting and to shorten the time of our own deployment.

265. The artillery of the main body first gives the necessary stability to the battle line that is being formed. In the long range and powerful effect of the artillery, the commander of the troops has the principal and most effective means to force his will upon the enemy.

It is the task of the artillery: to break the enemy's power of resistance, to open a road for the infantry, and to force the victory in conjunction with the infantry. This is the highest task of the artillery -all details serve this purpose.

Rapidity of reconnaissance and deployment enables the artillery to timely support the infantry.

On the other hand, the infantry takes into account the limitations of artillery and only makes such demands on the artillery that the latter can perform. Infantry, acting without due regard to artillery, injures itself.

The estimate of the terrain and recommendations for the employment of the artillery- which the division artillery commander submits in general outline to the division commander as soon as possible- takes into due account cooperation with the infantry and increasing the difficulties of hostile aerial reconnaissance. Insufficient view of the terrain and too great an extension of the artillery line can, when the division artillery is concentrated under the division artillery commander, endanger the proper support of the infantry, and therefore, it may be advisable to attach portions of the short range artillery to the infantry units early in the fight.

266. Based on the general situation, a personal estimate of the terrain and on the recommendations of the artillery commander, the division commander decides where the main body will be employed and at what point the center of gravity of the battle will be laid.

/en

The deployment, in accordance with the intentions of the division commander, is attained by timely assignment of march objectives to the portions of the main body drawn out of the march column.

Portions of the main body may be held back temporarily until the situation clears.

The first orders to the division artillery commander contain only the general plan and the general duties of the artillery. Detailed orders concerning attack objectives are issued only after first contact has clarified the situation. Until then, a portion of the artillery is held in reserve. Sufficient observation planes are now attached to the artillery.

It is the duty of the artillery commander of the division to take proper measures for reconnaissance and observation, to deploy his artillery in good time, to take measures for communication within his artillery and with the infantry, and to insure proper ammunition supply. The artillery is not crowded together in a limited space nor placed into position along broad lines. The batteries are distributed according to the terrain, organized in depth, and protected from aerial observation.

267. Endeavor is always made to deploy the main body as a unit, and, corresponding to the general situation and plan.

Conduct of the battle is dependent as a rule on the celerity of and the measures taken by the artillery. Premature advance on the part of the infantry leads to unnecessary loss and also to reverses. But cases may occur in which the commander of troops is forced to throw into action portions of infantry and artillery as they arrive, assigning attack objectives without hesitation, in order to hold some success attained by the advance guard or to exploit it.

268. Proper orders are issued to the commander of the engineers for employment of his troops and for the necessary reconnaissances.

The staff officer in charge of the signal troops is informed of the general situation and plan, location of different headquarters, and receives orders for the employment of his troops.

Sanitary companies, combat train, and field train are not allowed to go beyond certain points at first. Locations for the hospital station and stations for slightly wounded are reconnoitered.

269. The command post of the commander of the troops, or at least the telephone station required therefor, is selected as soon as possible, in order to permit immediate establishment of telephone communication. It is important to plainly mark this location for airplane dropped messages.

270. The situation is clarified further during development prior to deployment. In addition to renewed aerial and cavalry reconnaissance and employment of artillery observation detachments inclusive of artillery airplanes and balloons, officers patrols accompanied by machine guns are sent out towards the enemy with definite tasks of reconnaissance and screening. These patrols never permit themselves to be led into participating in general reconnaissance tasks assigned to other arms and units. However, they establish connection with reconnaissance units of other arms, working in the same sector, and exchange information with them.

/jn

Thus march reconnaissance changes to battle reconnaissance. Battle reconnaissance determines the strength, distribution of forces, and weak points in the enemy's position. All scouts, especially the artillery observers and all staff officers, equipped with scissors telescopes, constantly watch the terrain. On exposed flanks, battle reconnaissance is also carried on by aircraft and cavalry. It includes ascertaining the location of hostile flanks, movements behind the hostile front, and location of his artillery.

During the course of the battle, battle reconnaissance is continued by all arms and begun anew, if necessary, since only in this way can all arms be properly employed.

271. An envelopment is more easily executed when the original direction of the march to the front leads towards the enemy's flank or rear.

It is more difficult to execute when the direction is given after deployment, or when it is executed by reserves that have been held back.

An envelopment executed by shifting troops in the leading line is possible only when the terrain is specially favorable or at night.

It is of great importance to keep motor truck columns in readiness to carry forward reserves for employment at the decisive moment.

273. Simultaneous envelopment of both flanks is the most effective, but requires greatly superior forces. It should never lead to splitting of forces.

274. The troops designated for the envelopment are made as strong as possible in order to provide for all sudden changes in the battle and to bring about a decisive success. The front of the enemy is attacked with weak forces. It is an art to estimate correctly the force that can handle the front and how strong to make the enveloping force.

275. When envelopment is impossible, there should not be any hesitation to attack frontally. Every frontal attack requires cooperation between infantry and artillery to a high degree. The commander of the troops attempts to gain absolute superiority in a frontal attack through correct formation in depth and width at the most favorable point (terrain, enemy's weak points) and when possible, attempts a local envelopment. Any successful frontal attack results in a penetration of the enemy's line, which is increased to a complete break through of the hostile position by pushing forward in the original attack direction and driving off the enemy's reserves. Counter attacks are always considered.

After penetration, the adjoining fronts of the enemy are attacked and rolled back. Only in this way will a penetration be turned into complete victory. The attacking troops push through as far as possible and leave the rolling back of the adjoining fronts to the reserves. When attacking troops face to either side, new fronts are established and this leads to failure of the attack.

276. When reconnaissance shows that the enemy has already occupied a position and appears to have decided on defense, the attacker plans his attack on thorough reconnaissance of the hostile position and all advantages offering for the attack.

To ascertain the location of the enemy's main position and to gain sufficient terrain for our deployment, it is necessary to drive back all advanced hostile detachments. Strong patrols reconnoiter all possibilities of

/en

approach towards the enemy, and ascertain where large terrain obstacles exist. Signal corps troops accompany these patrols and maintain communication to the rear either with or without wire.

All observations made by the front line and especially those made by the artillery are immediately reported to the commander of the troops. They are frequently of the utmost importance in the selection of the attack direction.

When the preparations of the enemy are not advanced, it should be considered whether the attack should be started immediately in order to prevent the enemy from bringing up reinforcements or enlarging his position. If necessary, the enemy is approached under cover of darkness.

EXECUTION OF THE ATTACK

277. When the commander decides to proceed to the attack directly from march column and development, so as not to lose the advantage of prompt action, he issues orders to the units as they arrive, or issues a complete attack order and designates to each unit its zone of action and its objective.

In smaller commands, zones of action are not designated, but a definite axis is laid down to govern the general direction of the attack or a guide line leading into one of the hostile flanks.

The attack must not be premature. In larger commands, as well as in an attack against an enemy deployed for defense, orders for taking up a position in readiness generally always precede the orders for attack and deployment for attack.

278. When going into position in readiness, the commanders ride ahead of the troops and reconnoiter routes of approach and localities for the position in readiness. These should be beyond the range of hostile fire effect and from the enemy's observation especially from the air. Large assemblages of troops and regular formations are avoided unless the nature of the terrain permits.

When the terrain is generally without cover, the infantry is placed in readiness at a great distance from the enemy and at considerable intervals. This is necessary even when the hostile artillery fire is neutralized by our artillery fire which rarely happens.

279. In a position in readiness, it is by no means necessary to place all troops on the same line. The troops that have arrived closer to the enemy by favor of the terrain, can make it easier for the troops farther in rear to move forward over open ground. In case of need, points in front of the position of readiness are seized by quick attack; this refers to points necessary or important for observation and subsequent deployment.

280. Under difficult conditions, especially when the terrain cannot be overlooked, and at night, it may be advisable to bring the units up from one line to another, in order to preserve uniformity of advance into the position in readiness. The measures therefore are taken so that little time is lost by an advance from one line to another.

/en

281. When the division commander issues orders for the cessation of advance guard work, the artillery of the advance guard reports to the division artillery commander for orders unless it is attached to infantry units.

282. Thereafter and corresponding to the slow and regular deployment of the infantry comes the uniform employment of the bulk of the artillery. Its first tasks are to protect the infantry while going into position in readiness, to protect the positions, and then to protect the deployment.

In the subsequent course of the action, it is necessary for success, that definite battle missions be given the artillery by the commander of the troops, without interfering with the execution of them. The activity of the infantry and of the artillery is never separated in battle in the matter of either time or space. It is the duty of the highest commander to keep them constantly in accord.

Whether or not the artillery of the division may be separated in the beginning into short range and long range artillery, depends on its strength, the general situation, and the terrain. Short range artillery is distributed according to the distribution of the infantry. In taking up a position in readiness preceding an attack, it is exceptional to instruct short range artillery to report to the infantry commander for orders; but never hesitate to place the artillery under the orders of the infantry commander in any case where the close terrain and excessive extension of front and strength of artillery makes it questionable whether the division artillery commander can make timely arrangements himself for the proper artillery support of the infantry.

In any case the infantry always needs its accompanying batteries, which are under the direct orders of the infantry regimental commanders. They in turn may assign them by platoons or by pieces to different battalions, which in turn again assign them to companies for definite purposes. It is the task of infantry batteries from the beginning of the battle and in conjunction with the other heavy auxiliary arms of infantry, to break local resistance, to silence single hostile machine guns, machine gun groups, trench mortars and field pieces. This is best accomplished by frequent change of position and frequently moving forward single field pieces in the open; they quickly solve their task before drawing the hostile artillery fire on themselves. For this reason and also on account of difficulties in replenishing ammunition, these pieces are not suited for a long continued fire fight but rapidly disappear as soon as they have solved a certain task.

If, in addition to infantry batteries, also short range artillery is attached to infantry then this artillery, under orders of its artillery commander, engages those hostile targets that are most annoying to the infantry, in which case, concentrated fire will always produce the best effect. During the course of the battle, it may again become necessary to break up some of this artillery to solve some task or other in the manner of infantry batteries.

The short range artillery, placed under orders of the infantry commander always remains in communication with the division artillery commander, so that the latter is able at all times- pursuant to orders from the division commander- to concentrate the artillery effect on other targets.

283. The long range artillery hinders the activity of hostile artillery and employs harassing fire at long range on hostile movements and other good targets.

/en

284. The artillery attempts to perform all tasks given it without changing position. Changing position interrupts effect. In many instances, the object can be attained by merely shifting observation posts. But change of position is made without delay when greater or quicker effect is expected from a position closer to the enemy or from a position that flanks the enemy. Any change of position is executed by sections (echelons).

In the first reconnaissance, the selection of the position is governed by the possibility of laying a concentrated artillery fire on the decisive points. Long range flat trajectory fire is used to protect exposed flanks.

Artillery itself is protected by the infantry in its front. Special protection is necessary only on exposed flanks. The division artillery commander takes the necessary security measures. But its own alertness protects the artillery against surprises. Each battery or artillery unit is prepared for self-defense.

285. After the position in readiness has been completely taken up, the commander of the troops issues his orders for the attack.

By assigning definite sectors for deployment and assigning attack objectives to the infantry, there are created certain zones of action of varying width. By making these zones of action narrow, the commander of the troops has the simplest means in his hands of increasing the depth of the formation at the decisive point and thus carry out his plan. It is always well to designate a base unit to which all other units conform in their movements.

286. Concerning spaces for deployment, calculations are based on the general rule, that for any attack by a division composed of three infantry regiments and plenty of artillery, 3 to 4 kilometers are required on a terrain favorable for all arms. This width is increased by employing the force in groups and by leaving gaps in the front. But if this method is carried too far, it not only becomes difficult to direct the fight, but makes it difficult to increase the depth of formations at the decisive point. Definite rules cannot be laid down for the width of the deployment of the several units. The width of a battalion protected on both flanks will, as a general rule, vary from 500 to 800 meters. Mission, fighting strength, terrain, and artillery support from our own or neighboring sector always exert a certain influence.

When calculating on the strength, use the established rule, that forces can never be too strong at the decisive point. But the field of battle should never be so overcrowded that, even after material casualties, some units can never get into action.

287. The units move into the deployment spaces along reconnoitered routes. Patrols are sent ahead. When necessary, the route is marked taking advantage of all dead spaces. When terrain offers cover, the march column is employed as a general rule. When there is no cover in the terrain, single groups are formed and dispersed irregularly. They make the best use of the terrain by frequently changing their formations. Broad and dense skirmish lines are avoided.

lkb

At completion of the deployment, each unit must be in its assigned zone of action and opposite and as close to its point of attack as possible. This requires plenty of space in width and depth.

Any unit designated for envelopment is started with lateral intervals so that the interior flanks of the troops attacking frontally and of the enveloping troops do not interfere during the attack.

288. Execution of the infantry attack, after sufficient frontal reconnaissance, consists in carrying forward the light arms of the infantry (rifles, light machine guns, automatic pistols, grenade throwers), while supported by the artillery of the division, heavy machine guns and trench mortars. The latter are timely placed into position, so that they can cover the field of attack; for this purpose their commanders hasten on ahead.

The infantry batteries are kept so close that they can go quickly into position when required. In very close terrain, or when the battle changes into fighting by smaller groups, it is generally best to place single heavy machine guns or machinegun platoons under the orders of the infantry commanders in the furthest advanced firing line. This is done not later than just before the intended penetration of the hostile position, or for the continuation of the attack.

Fire is opened as late as practicable, so that ammunition is not wasted at ineffective ranges and so that time is not lost. The distance for opening of fire depends on the terrain, the hostile fire effect, and last but not least on the efficiency of our troops.

The skirmishers take cover at irregular intervals and distances, around their squad leaders, making extensive use of the spade. The subsequent advance of the infantry is made by squad rushes, by several men together, or by individuals. Squads rushing forward are never without fire support. While one squad rushes forward the neighboring squads, heavy machine guns, trench mortars and when necessary field pieces, hold down the hostile fire. In this phase, independence on the part of subordinate commanders is very necessary.

It is of decisive importance to the outcome of the attack that the infantry be supported by artillery and that the infantry take immediate advantage of the artillery effect. As soon as our infantry approaches the effective range of the hostile infantry fire, the mass of our artillery, including the long range artillery, turns its fire on the hostile infantry.

The artillery fire is generally delivered in bursts for longer or shorter continuing periods.

While the infantry works its way to an assaulting distance, the artillery increases the volume of its fire. Finally, it places its greatest concentration of fire on the point designated by the commander of the troops, to shake those portions of the hostile infantry that are still fit for offering resistance. Artillery airplanes and artillery liaison officers endeavor to rapidly place the artillery fire on the principal points of the battle. The fire of the mass of the heavy infantry arms is directed against those points.

lkb

The artillery, by directing its fire on the point of the hostile position, that is to be entered, gives the infantry confidence and assurance in the success of the attack. When it appears that the enemy is sufficiently shaken, then the assault is launched.

It depends on conditions, whether the assault is initiated by the foremost portions of the troops or orders therefore emanate from the commander of the troops. When the foremost troops have gained the impression that the time is ripe for the decision, they should not hesitate to hazard the assault. They should, however, have assurance that the artillery fire will be shifted.

When the enemy is formed in deep formation, the resistance of his supporting points is broken one after the other. Then the assault assumes the form of a succession of separate fights, eating through the zone of hostile resistance, in the course of which the artillery participates with full effect. This holds especially for the artillery placed under the orders of the infantry (infantry batteries and short range artillery).

The assaulting squads work their way forward supporting one another. The fire of all arms annihilates the machine gun nests and the supporting points; the squads that have pushed forward farthest support their neighboring squads by flank and enveloping fire.

Flanks and rear are protected by units following. All rear detachments and reserves are rapidly pushed forward through the fighting zone, so as to quickly replace our casualties.

Counter attacks are considered; for repulsing them, it is necessary to have mutual support by machine gun and skirmish squads, timely artillery fire, fire of the heavy infantry arms, and rapid use of reserves.

289. The artillery strives to observe the time when the infantry starts the assault, by using all available means to keep the leading infantry units in sight. When this is impossible and when the time of the assault is not regulated by orders or previous agreement, then in most cases, the infantry will notify the artillery that it is about to assault. Single rockets at one point and another are soon followed by numerous signals appearing all along the line. The sum total thereof causes the artillery to increase its fire to the utmost and to lengthen the range, turning occasionally into barrage fire. At this moment of great tension, the most exact cooperation between the two arms is of the utmost importance. While the artillery lays down a rolling barrage, the infantry must without fear of casualties follow up its own artillery fire without distance. At this moment, the artillery and the infantry planes are started out. These airplanes by means of wireless and visual signals, are capable of maintaining proper communication between infantry and artillery.

290. As soon as the assault is started, all reserves still in rear are brought forward. Either on orders received, or by their knowledge of the situation, some of the batteries arrange for change of position, and then hasten forward. These batteries annihilate portions of the enemy still holding out, prevent counter-attacks and by sharp pursuit fire insure the exploitation of success. At the same time, all available attack airplanes participate in the battle on the ground.

/lkb

291. When the entire front of the enemy is shaken, victory is near. If the enemy succeeds in taking up a new position or in preparing for renewed resistance in positions in rear, he is again attacked. Reserves coming up are thrown into the battle to prevent the attack from coming to a standstill, repulse counter attacks and to carry everything forward. Even if by doing so, the center of gravity of the action is shifted, the reserves are employed where some success has been attained so as to immediately take advantage thereof in full force. Detachments that have become separated and stragglers are quickly assembled and employed. They follow up the attack farther in rear. Weak security detachments are left in the position that was taken first. And thus, the final resistance of the enemy is broken and the road opened for pursuing the enemy beyond the battle field.

292. When, after a successful attack, forces are insufficient for continuing the attack, they at least hold the terrain that has been taken. The skirmishers, formed in great depth, closely hug the ground; intrench themselves, construct strong points, and await the arrival of reinforcements to continue the forward movement. The artillery fire, newly regulated, gives necessary protection to the infantry. This regulation of the artillery fire not only comprises the defense from hostile infantry attacks but also holds down the hostile artillery fire which is so severe on the infantry in this situation.

The artillery also secures the terrain captured when darkness ends the battle before an assault is made. Artillery and trench mortars find the range by trial shots before darkness sets in.

293. If in a meeting engagement, frontal attack against the enemy does not bring a decision, consideration is given to a change in formation, during the night, to assure success of the attack at some other point.

lkb

## VII. PURSUIT.

294. The victor pursues on a broad front, always endeavoring to outflank the enemy, to overtake him, and to get ahead of him.

295. In most situations, the commander of the troops is able to perceive the intentions of the enemy to start the retreat by reports from his aerial forces, from his troops, from the fact that his troops are pushing forward victoriously, from the fact that the hostile resistance diminishes, and occasionally also from reports from neighboring detachments. By immediately informing his subordinate commanders thereof, he spurs them on to victory, and by shifting the remaining reserves and by forming new reserves, he throws the pursuit into the desired direction.

As soon as the enemy gives way in their front, subordinate commanders without waiting for orders and without delay, and without regard to whether their troops are exhausted, start the pursuit of the beaten enemy. They act audaciously and independently. This is the more justified, because the enemy has but one intention, and that is to evade the victor. Frequently it is not possible to reestablish order and cohesion in units, nor to bring up ammunition and subsistence until the forward movement has begun, so as not to delay the relentless pursuit. Fresh troops arriving are used without delay.

The entire aerial fighting forces attack the hostile main body regardless of their original aerial tasks. By machine gun fire and bombs, they increase the dissolution of the enemy and cause confusion among the traffic on the roads to the rear and at the railroad stations.

The observation squadrons are used to ascertain the enemy's route of retreat.

296. The best means to fully exploit a victory is to correctly employ the artillery. Artillery is specially suited for pursuit as it combines rapidity of movement with long range fire power. It, therefore, relentlessly gathers the fruits of the victory and employs every available gun at effective range. Hostile tanks advancing for counter attack are rapidly annihilated by the artillery. Portions of the artillery, especially the long range batteries, remain as long in their positions as the enemy can be effectively damaged with observed fire, balloon observation being used as far as possible. Other portions of the artillery pursue the enemy in conjunction with the infantry, and still others join the columns that are to overtake the fleeing enemy. For the latter task, horse artillery, artillery on motor trucks, cavalry and other mobile units are specially suited.

The artillery in the front lines fighting frequently fires on the most distant portions of the enemy, in order to bring confusion there also. Long range guns, firing on the route of retreat and railroad stations find there a paying field of activity.

Frequently there is not time to issue orders for change of position. Subordinate artillery commanders act on their own decision. Artillery observers, following the enemy with the most advanced infantry, attempt to keep in communication with their batteries by wireless.

ms

Prerequisite for successful pursuit is sufficient ammunition; all commanders make arrangements therefor; employment of motor truck trains for bringing up ammunition is advisable.

297. All infantry not designated for overtaking pursuit, stays on the heels of the enemy. By fire and relentless forward movement, the defeat of the enemy is increased to annihilation. When the enemy evades the pursuing fire effect, every effort is made to get closer to him and to attack with cold steel.

Attached short range batteries, infantry batteries, and trench mortars advance in close conjunction with the infantry and go into position immediately in rear of the infantry, and frequently in the open. Machine guns are in the foremost ranks. Full utilization is made of motor trucks to carry the infantry and the machine guns forward. In many instances, cyclist units and armored automobiles can be effectively used.

Lines of communication follow up the leading infantry units. The subordinate infantry commanders frequently report to division headquarters concerning the situation; division headquarters is always in wireless communication with them.

The enemy's rear guards are never permitted to divertthe pursuer from the correct direction and are never allowed to pin down stronger pursuing detachments. The pursuer manages to push through the rearguards, or go around them, in order to reach the hostile main body as soon as possible.

298. The pursuit is limited only by direct orders from highest headquarters. The pursuit never stops in front of a defensive sector.

ms

## VIII. BREAKING OFF A BATTLE. RETREAT.

299. If, after thorough consideration, the commander perceives that the battle holds no hope whatever of decisive success and that continuation thereof will only cause useless casualties which are in no relation whatever to the purpose of the battle, then, in full knowledge of his responsibility, he will break off the battle.

The situation, plan, and terrain determines the time for withdrawing the troops.

In almost all cases it is necessary to wait until night. The main question is to hold out in a difficult situation until dark.

300. It is easiest to break off a battle just after a local success. It is better accomplished, the more we succeed in hiding our intention therefor, and becomes the more difficult the farther the battle progresses.

301. At first the infantry, organized in depth, tenaciously holds its positions. Supported to the utmost by the entire artillery, machine guns, trench mortars, and attack airplanes, the single groups fall back at a walk; penetration is prevented by counter attacks. Wherever possible, breathing space is gained by flanking fire, otherwise by charging with cold steel.

302. In the meantime, the highest headquarters make all arrangements for the retreat. By means of the map, it locates a new position, designates its garrison and sectors, assigns routes of retreat to the different units, starts combat and field trains towards their new location, reconnoiters the new position and roads leading thereto, requires the engineers to throw bridges where needed, and to arrange for demolition of bridges. The sanitary units receive timely orders for the evacuation of wounded. Efficient officers are immediately sent out to see that the roads for the retreat are kept clear.

303. Signal corps units are sent ahead to establish communication. At nightfall, the troops are disengaged from the enemy. They fall back first on a broad front and organized in great depth, using all available roads. Gradually the different units are assigned to the roads designated for their retreat and march columns are formed. When the new position is far in rear, it is well to establish a rallying position on the flank of the line of retreat with reserves reinforced with artillery. These forces subsequently follow as rearguard into the new position.

The troops left engaged with the enemy are withdrawn when the departure of the main body is assured, and when the necessary start is gained. Armored automobiles perform valuable service in this connection.

The last troops generally disengage themselves from the enemy along the entire front. Patrols, composed of fearless men and plentifully supplied with ammunition, light signals, machine guns, armored automobiles, and single field pieces, screen the retreat by stratagem, by fighting where necessary. In making these final stands the loss of some guns is not considered.

ms

Proper arrangements are made for protection from hostile pursuing planes.

Overtaking pursuit on the part of the enemy is met by flank guards.

304. As soon as the retreat is assured, the commander of the troops hastens to the vicinity where renewed resistance is to be made in order to make all necessary arrangements there.

All subordinate commanders remain with their units during the retreat.

305. During the course of the further retreat, it is the endeavor of the commander of the troops to increase the distance between his troops and the enemy, and thereby again secure freedom of action.

Increased marches, early starts, night marches, and far reaching measures against attack from the air are recommended.

Using available railroads is possible, only when proper preparations are made in advance. The use of railroads is made difficult for the enemy by employing attack airplanes, especially directed against his detraining stations.

306. As soon as the troops are disengaged from the enemy, a rear guard is formed corresponding to the organization of the troops. It is the task of the rear guard to secure the main body against interference and attack. The necessary time therefor is gained by forcing the enemy to deploy by long range artillery and machine gun fire, and without employing very much infantry; and after the enemy deploys the troops, march off unperceived. The mounted arms and the cyclist troops are the last to leave. They are able through their greater mobility to catch up with the marching infantry. But sometimes portions of infantry are left near the enemy with the mounted arms up to the last moment, and their mobility then increased by the use of motor truck columns.

307. When the enemy pursues sharply, stronger resistance is offered even when there is danger of suffering heavy casualties. The rear guard must never hesitate to attack, being supported by armored cars, so as to procure a sufficient start for the main body. Attacking a carelessly pursuing enemy is always advisable, if for no other than moral reasons.

308. Relentless employment of aerial forces is a material help in breaking the enemy's will to be victorious.

309. The rear guard falls back from one line to another. To delay the pursuing enemy, roads and bridges and remaining wire communications are destroyed. Railroads are blocked and interrupted. Orders for destruction of railroads and wireless traffic are issued only by the commander in chief.

310. The rear guard commander maintains communication with the commander of the main body. He uses existing telephone lines therefor.

ms

Wireless communication is limited to the lowest requirements in order to prevent the enemy from gaining any information by listening-in. In calculating the distance to be maintained between main body and rear guard, the commander of the latter reckons with delays in the march of the former and necessary halts for rest.

When the conduct of the enemy no longer necessitates march in battle deployment, the rear guard also assumes the march column.

ms

## IX. ATTACK ON POSITIONS

### A. IN OPEN SITUATIONS.

311. When the enemy awaits the attack in a terrain reinforced by field fortifications, one must consider that he employs only weaker forces there in order to have stronger forces in readiness and available at some other point.

In such a case, the attacker considers whether he can circumvent the position or whether it is necessary to attack it. In the former case, advantage is taken of darkness.

312. The strength of fortified positions varies according to whether they were hastily constructed or constructed after days of work with all available means at hand.

313. For that reason the method of attack will differ. Frequently a position can be approached only during the night. By the fact that the defender temporarily declines freedom of action, he permits the attacker to make thorough preparations.

314. Reconnaissance is increased during the march, and officers of all arms participate therein. Uniform conduct of reconnaissance hastens and increases the value of results. Hostile advanced positions, extension of the main position, as well as distribution of forces, are ascertained as far as possible.

Airplanes and balloons perform valuable services in this reconnaissance. Appearing early and in front of the position, they find the opponent still employed in construction and, can by sight and by taking aerial photos, gain a complete view of situation, location, and method of reinforcing the terrain. Artillery and engineer officers also reconnoiter from aircraft.

Efforts are made from the beginning to gain superiority of the air.

Systematic and continuous observation of the hostile ground and wireless communications, listening in on his telephone lines by listening-in stations, produce valuable information concerning the organization and strength of the enemy.

Reconnaissance by mounted patrols in front soon ceases; the more important then becomes mounted reconnaissance on the flanks and dismounted reconnaissance in the front.

Well planned establishment of all means of communication, especially construction of lateral lines to neighboring detachments is arranged for in good time.

315. Exact knowledge of the enemy is generally gained, only after the hostile advanced troops have been driven back. This, therefore, is accomplished as early as possible. But the attacking troops are not crowded together in front of the hostile advanced positions. Only as much

infantry as is absolutely necessary is employed, the remainder of the infantry never allows itself to be diverted from its original march direction by the hostile advanced troops. On the other hand, employment of strong artillery is generally necessary.

316. The attacker at the same time takes possession of the terrain from which he has a good view into the battle position, and which he requires for his observation positions and deployment of his artillery.

The mass of our infantry does not at first cross the limits of the hostile effective artillery fire; it is well to develop the infantry.

317. After completion of these introductory measures, further reconnaissance of the hostile main position, of our routes of approach, of the attack terrain and battery positions with observation stations commences. The time, therefor is not calculated too sparingly so that proper measures can be taken, based on more definite reports. Subsequent changes consume time and are frequently impossible.

It is sometimes necessary to lead the enemy into betraying his position by sending out strong infantry and engineer detachments, accompanied by machine guns, and artillery.

Aerial reconnaissance sends in more and more details. These details are best shown by aerial photographs, which gain their highest value only when supplemented by ground reconnaissance. Liberal distribution of aerial photos to the troops materially facilitates the ground reconnaissance.

Of special importance is early and uniform reconnaissance of targets by airplanes, balloons and artillery observation groups. This reconnaissance frequently furnishes the basis for the employment and fire control of artillery.

Message centers are established; listening posts sent ahead.

318. After the situation is cleared up, the commander of the troops decides whether or not he can take the hostile position by envelopment. Such a move is always attempted. Prior to the start of the envelopment, the hostile front is attacked however, to prevent the enemy from shifting his forces.

When the enemy is protected on both flanks, or when an envelopment is impossible for other reasons, the frontal attack is executed, which leads to penetration and subsequent break-through. In this matter, the main point is for the commander of the troops to perceive the weakness of the hostile front and to direct his attack against that point. It is seldom correct to distribute forces equally along the entire front; the infantry is preferably concentrated against one or more points of entry, while only minor forces are started against other points, or while some of the sectors of the hostile position are left undisturbed. Distribution of the artillery is based on this consideration also; concentrating superior fire does not mean concentrated position.

ms

Narrow points of penetration are not selected, because they subject troops to concentrated hostile artillery fire.

319. The artillery of the attacker goes into position under protection of the advanced infantry. When opposed by hostile artillery ready for action, this method is employed with great caution. Formation in width and depth corresponds to terrain conditions and observation conditions. Preparations for observation, fire control, opening of fire, and protection against aerial and ground observation, is not made too hastily; the necessary time is allowed the artillery.

As a general rule, it is not advisable in the interest of uniform fire preparation, to attach short range batteries in addition to the regular infantry batteries to the infantry attacking fortified field positions. Whether or not it is advisable, as early as the approach march to separate the artillery into long range and short range artillery, depends on the strength of the artillery and conditions with the enemy.

420. Efforts are made to have the artillery open fire simultaneously. But that is not always possible. Portions of the artillery are sometimes able to go into position only under the fire protection of other portions. It is also advisable to hold out some batteries to employ by surprise against hostile artillery that has not been seen in the beginning. All airplanes and balloons placed under the orders of the artillery commander, are employed in observing the trial shots for range, and watching the fire for effect; and other means of observation (ground reconnaissance, flash and sound ranging units) are also used. The main requirement for this latter is careful arrangement of wire communications.

It is the task of the artillery to break the enemy's resistance and thus open a road for the infantry. For that purpose, the artillery first of all cripples the hostile artillery so that our infantry can cross the hostile fire zone. Later on and while the defenders artillery is being held down, portions of the long range artillery concentrate their fire with that of the short range artillery and the heavy infantry arms, against the portions of the position that are considered most important by the commander of the troops according to the terrain and plans. Gas shells are used not only against artillery, but against important supporting points such as villages and woods.

It must be considered that the defender may not have fully occupied the position with his infantry, or only by weak forces, as long as our infantry attack has not yet made itself felt, and that therefore, artillery fire on the works is justifiable only when it is seen that particular defensive work is occupied. The artillery effect is strongest when simultaneous advance and attack on the part of our infantry compels the defender to occupy his works and show his troops. For that reason, the commander of the troops attempts to bring the gradual deployment of the infantry into harmony with the protection offered by the artillery fire.

As the infantry attack progresses, larger portions of the artillery receive short range tasks and, to increase the support of infantry in its increasingly difficult task, portions of the short range

ms

batteries are now placed under the orders of the infantry commander. The independence of these short range artillery battalions and batteries must result in closer and closer coöperation of the two arms.

321. Only when sufficiently supported by the artillery can the infantry get close enough to the hostile position in daytime to seek a decision before the approach of darkness.

322. When the attack cannot be finished within one day, the succeeding night is employed to bring the infantry close to the enemy.

The infantry in that case, intrenches itself deep, at points where it is forced to halt. It then gradually works its way forward at different points and intrenches again. In this creeping forward, machine guns, trench mortars and field pieces assist in force. In case of need, several nights are used to work up to an assault position.

323. The opponent is kept in the dark as much as possible as to the intentions of the attacker, the time the assault is to start, and the selected point of penetration, by keeping him busy along his entire front.

Traffic of the enemy in and in rear of the position, especially bringing up reserves, for the decision, is made as difficult as possible by throwing on harassing fire deep into the terrain. Cooperation of airplanes materially increases the chances of success of a well prepared attack.

324. In most cases the commander of the troops states the time of the assault. Frequently the assault is started at the break of day. It is always preceded by strong preparation by artillery and trench mortars. The assault immediately follows the artillery bombardment in order to take full advantage of its effect.

Considering that as a general rule the defenders infantry is in deep formation, the assault generally changes into separate fights. The means of overcoming the defender are found, in continuously feeding the battle from the depth at the decisive point, in taking proper care of the flanks of the troops working their way through the enemy; the counter thrusts and counter attacks of the defender are at all times encountered by alert artillery, fighting troops and reserves.

325. Further advance in the previous direction, at first for the purpose of capturing the hostile artillery, is the next task of the attacking infantry. The reserves also, following close in rear, push into the depth of the position. Prematurely turning towards a flank weakens the decisive shock and decreases chances of complete success.

The captured position is garrisoned by a security detachment and prepared for defense to prevent reverses.

Pursuit is started as rapidly as possible.

326. When a frontal attack against a fortified field position is undecisive, it is considered in how far a complete change in the forma-

ms

tion of the troops during the night will favor success of the attack at some other point.

## B. ATTACK IN STABILIZED SITUATIONS.

327. In a protracted stabilized situation, the attack generally encounters a defensive system of field fortifications that has been constructed with thorough consideration and by employment of all possible means, and which cannot be enveloped. Here, surprising the enemy is of even greater importance than in open situations. On the other hand, the opponent holding a prepared position always takes proper counter measures. Therefore special measures are necessary for screening our true intentions and deceiving the enemy. But nevertheless it is difficult to keep secret the place and time of attack. Therefore, frequent changes in the method of attack are made in order to continually place new tasks before the defender.

328. The main blow strikes the enemy's most vulnerable and sensitive point, and shakes the hostile line along a broad front by means of the direction given the attack. Open terrain without too many defensive lines is best. After successful penetration, it facilitates the utilization of all advantages of open situations, and therefore increases the enemy's difficulties in rapid construction of a new continuous defensive front.

329. Besides strategical considerations, local tactical conditions and location of the intended penetration governs the selection of the attack front. Here also, the terrain is of the greatest importance for the full employment of means for the attack. The main point is for the attacker to rapidly take possession of the dominating terrain and penetrate deeper and deeper into the hostile position, while reserves follow and roll up the hostile flanks, on each side of the penetration.

330. Considering the importance tanks play as an offensive arm in stabilized situations, their correct employment is carefully thought out in both the selection of the point of attack as well as in the execution of the attack.

In order not to prematurely betray the approach of tanks by their unusually loud noise, special measures are necessary (noise of battle, artillery fire near the tanks, etc).

331. In no instance, is an attack at some one point able to do without the cooperation of other sectors. It is the task of these latter to divert and hold material forces of the enemy from the main attack by offensive operations, even if only with limited objectives, small forces, or by other measures (deceiving movements, deceiving the enemy by sending false wireless messages, etc).

332. The more carefully and systematically preparations for the attack are made, the greater are the chances of success.

Plans and time of attack are kept from the troops as long as possible.

### PREPARATIONS FOR THE ATTACK.

333. The zone of action of a division of three infantry regiments,

as a general rule, does not exceed 2½ kilometers in width. The offensive means required by the division, especially technical troops, wagon and motor truck columns, ammunition, subsistence, equipment and tools of all kinds, and the time necessary to bring these up, are generally very important, and are accurately calculated. Strong artillery and trench mortar units are attached for preparing the hostile works for the assault, and numerous heavy and light tank units are also attached.

334. Thorough preparations require the following:

Location of command posts and extension of the communicating lines. Every newly arriving division finds a telephone net already prepared for its use.

Careful regulation and screening of the information traffic.

Shelter and supply of water.

Good cover for reserves and tanks.

Construction of numerous battery positions well forward for the reinforcing artillery. Reconnaissance of routes of approach. Designation of the new organization of troops; the targets, as well as the spaces for the annihilating fire; location of observation stations. Extension of the artillery command and information net. Reconnaissance and measurement of ranges from battery positions for the advancing artillery up to the line of outposts. Construction of repair shops.

Shelter for and employment of our aerial forces. Antiaircraft measures.

Assurance of sufficient ammunition supply and rations for all attacking units. Organization of attacking units.

Location of ammunition storage, parks, subsistence depots, etc. are merely enlarged or newly constructed.

Thoroughly testing the capacity of all railroads, inclusive of field railroads and tramways; enlarging their capacity in case of need.

Construction of a good and sufficient road net. Each division has a main route of approach; traffic coming from the front uses neighboring roads or goes across country.

Care of wounded; shelter for main dressing stations and field hospitals for the newly arriving divisions and army sanitary units; increase in the number of motorized ambulances; placing hospital trains in readiness; emptying the hospitals; reinforcing and enlarging the assembly stations for the sick; augmenting sanitary supplies.

335. Further consideration is given to the service of supply and the conduct of it after the attack has been successful. To overcome shell-craters, trenches and watercourses, numerous engineer and road construction companies with all necessary materials are required. Arrangements are made for the subsequent use of establishments left by the

ms

enemy, especially combining the roads and railroads found there with our own road net.

336. During preparations, nothing is permitted to attract the attention of the enemy. For that reason, no change occurs in normal fighting activities. The service of communication receives no changes whatever. Specially selected officers supervise the cautious execution of all the preparations.

The greatest caution is necessary against observation from hostile airplanes. Necessary works and movements are generally made at night in order to deceive the enemy. Any kind of arrangement indicating attack, every concentration of troops is concealed from the hostile airplanes. Our airplanes daily watch our own positions and the terrain in rear. Airplanes and balloons report immediately and directly to the commander of troops, anything of our preparations that is seen by them and which might give some hint to the hostile airplanes. During the night, balloons watch the deployment area for fires showing in the bivouacs and for lights in houses and along roads and streets.

Screening railroad traffic by running troop trains only at night, is feasible only on stretches near terminals.

337. In spite of all screening measures to keep the enemy and our own troops in the dark, reconnaissance of the enemy, of the entire attack terrain as well as adjoining terrain is continued. Besides using the means offered by the intelligence service for this reconnaissance, the ground and aerial reconnoitering means are cautiously employed. It is often even necessary to start minor operations to bring in some prisoners.

The following is ascertained:

Location of the hostile infantry positions, main line of resistance, strong points, obstacles, command posts, movements of the hostile infantry; artillery positions, observation stations, ammunition depots and parks, shifting of hostile artillery; railroad works and facilities, lines of communication, construction of roads, airdromes, balloons, shelters, especially those of headquarters, camps, parks, routes of approach, together with what has been previously observed and paying due attention to false and misleading works.

All results of reconnaissances are marked on maps and battery sketches, and that work is kept up to date even during the attack. Timely distribution of these maps and specially of aerial photos to the attacking troops is of special importance.

338. The divisions designated to execute the attack send the following officers in good time to general headquarters; the first general staff officer, artillery commanders, aerial commanders, engineer commanders, information officers, telephone officers, commanders of the trains and motor truck columns.

339. The approach march of the attack divisions is thoroughly prepared. Marches, shelters, and time when the attack divisions take

ms

over control of the sectors from divisions in line are exactly stated.

340. Deployment of the artillery requires special consideration. In consideration of the matter of surprise, it is made rapidly without lessening security and subsequent effect.

In the face of a strongly intrenched enemy, the attacking power of infantry lasts longer, the further the artillery opens a road for it. Therefore the artillery goes into position as far to the front as practicable. In most cases, success is attained by keeping down a material portion of the hostile artillery from the very start, the capture of which is the first task of the infantry after entering the position.

Considering the large number of batteries of the reinforcing artillery arriving, it is advisable to reinforce the artillery of the front line divisions even before the artillery deployment proper. But the mass of the reinforcing batteries does not go into position earlier than the last few nights prior to the attack.

Finding the range by trial shots is omitted, as that immediately betrays our intentions.

341. As the appearance of strong aerial forces and the increase in number of airdromes betrays to the enemy our attack intentions, special measures are required to give the aerial units designated for the attack, the necessary knowledge of the terrain, in spite of their late arrival at the front. Balloons are not shown either. Superiority in the air is gained at the opening of the attack.

342. The line of departure from which the assault is started is occupied the last night preceding the assault.

THE ATTACK

343. Artillery and trench mortar fire is centrally controlled within the units as a whole at the opening of the attack. When a majority of the divisions designated for the attack take up the line of departure during the night preceding the attack, correct fire control is not assured by delegating this matter, to one of these divisions.

344. In most cases, the artillery fire is first of all directed against the hostile artillery, special works in the infantry positions, and long range targets. This is done for the purpose of; crippling the hostile artillery activities, silencing the more important defensive works, interrupting the activity of all headquarters and interfering with traffic on the roads in rear. The duration of this fire depends on general conditions. Gas shells are used against; firing positions, camps, and certain localities not offering a clear view, such as probable assembly places of reserves. Gas is also used against obstacles that are not crossed by the attacking troops, to form gas barrages for flank protection and for locking in trenches.

Later, the fire is directed against the hostile infantry positions by throwing a concentrated destructive fire on the enemy's known main points of resistance. Trench mortars participate in the

ms

artillery preparatory fire. Observation of the hits of the massed fire and the newly appearing targets by airplanes and balloons is well regulated. The fire is interrupted by irregular fire pauses in order to induce the enemy to occupy his positions and to keep him in uncertainty as to the actual time of the attack. During the bombardment of the hostile infantry positions, the hostile artillery is held down.

The enemy's road traffic, routes of approach, railroads and detraining stations are interrupted by long range fire.

In advance prepared artillery and trench mortar maps, the distribution of fire for each single phase of the battle is accurately shown.

When the infantry attack starts, all available batteries as a general rule lay a rolling barrage immediately in front of the infantry. In determining time of fire, which is regulated strictly according to synchronized watches, it should be remembered that the infantry will get forward only slowly, especially when the terrain is difficult.

Warning is given against adopting any kind of a fixed scheme for the artillery preparation. That preparation conforms to conditions existing at the time and is in the nature of a surprise for the enemy. To this method pertain: alternate fire with gas shells and ordinary shells; gas surprises and shell fire combined with gas attacks by means of "blowing" the gas.

345. To avoid losses, the penetration by the infantry into the hostile position is made not in lines but in deep formation, by dispersed groups and changeable formations adapted to the terrain; the main point being to bring forward as rapidly as possible a large fire power in the shape of numerous machine guns, trench mortars and infantry batteries. Formations in close order are employed only far in rear. The fighting and communication trenches are cleared by special cleaning-up squads. Detachments charged with consolidating captured strong points, and policing the battlefield, and labor squads which bring forward materials and fighting means, follow up the assaulting infantry.

346. Covering the entire attack terrain or portions thereof by smoke screens shortly prior to the assault, breaks up the hostile fire effect, hinders his observation and protects our troops at least against sight. But that method increases the difficulties of our own leadership and endangers the uniformity of our attacks. Conditions of wind are taken into account. A smoke screen is always desirable however, for deceiving purposes and for flank protection.

347. Tanks always fight in closest conjunction with infantry. Their position in readiness is concealed from the hostile aerial observers. After prior and careful terrain reconnaissance, they attack by surprise and as a unit. Employment in large numbers and great depth formation is necessary for lasting success; also a reserve is held out.

ms

Light tanks are attached by platoons to the infantry; the heavy tanks being employed against deep and strong defensive and flanking works. They precede the light tanks and open a road for the latter in shot up terrain. Light and heavy tanks are also kept back with the reserves to be subsequently employed with the reserves when the artillery fire support no longer suffices for protecting the infantry, because of the screening distance. The advance of tanks is screened by smoke.

The highest commander maintains a tank reserve for special battle purposes.

348. Although the fire of the entire artillery has been conducted as one unit, up to the time the barrage fire ceases, the divisional artillery and portions of the reinforcing artillery with observation detachments and trench mortar units are then promptly attached to the divisions. The divisions assign them places immediately in rear of the assaulting infantry. Engineer platoons, with proper materials, are made available for overcoming the shell-torn terrain and the terrain cut up by trenches.

In the further progress of the attack, the fire of hostile batteries echeloned far to the rear or that of newly appearing batteries is held down. Therefore, in its advance, the artillery maintains connection with its aerial observers. The heavy and heaviest flat trajectory guns work with aerial observation, remaining in their original positions up to the full limit of their range. Mobile flash and sound ranging squads are employed by the division.

The artillery and trench mortar units not assigned to divisions, form the reserve of the higher units (corps, artillery, army artillery, etc). Proper and early preparations are made so that they will be available for work at the decisive point of the attack and can carry forward the attack; however, unless ammunition is rapidly brought up, artillery is worthless. By establishing message centers with all means of communication, especially several wire lines to the rear, communication with the most advance fighting line is assured.

349. When there is reliable information or indications that the enemy will not accept the decision in the position heretofore held by him, and withdraws to a position in rear or assumes a greater depth formation in a mobile battlefield defense, then the attack is carried forward from sector to sector from the beginning. The supreme command directs in each instance the objectives to be reached by the infantry and leaves the divisions to bring the artillery rapidly forward by echelons within their combat sectors; he also decides whether the entire artillery or only portions thereof be left to the divisions for the continuation of the attack. Preparation is always made for hostile counter attacks.

350. Attacks without or after a very short artillery preparation are the exception. They promise success only by means of surprise and when made against an enemy who is already shaken. The lack of or insufficient artillery preparation is offset by the employment of numerous tanks.

ms

351. Prerequisite for participation of attack airplanes in the battle on the ground, is complete freedom of movement in the air.

When the enemy has had the superiority in the air up to the time of the attack because our pursuit squadrons were purposely held back, his superiority in the air is rapidly broken when the attack starts by surprise and concentrated attack just above the most important places of the battle on the ground.

Protected by the pursuit squadrons, the combat planes are repeatedly employed against the most important points along the hostile front. Their activities simultaneously with or directly after the infantry assault are specially effective.

During the subsequent course of the battle, the roads leading to the battlefield covered with troops and vehicles form the main points of attack for the attacking airplanes as well as for all other combat airplanes. Their principal objectives lie where the attacking infantry encounters material resistance and where it lacks artillery support. Bombing attacks are carried on day and night in the terrain in rear for the purpose of damaging the enemy.

## C. ATTACK AGAINST PERMANENT FORTIFICATIONS.

352. Localities and lines of fortifications arranged for defense in time of peace materially differ from strong field fortifications in the matter of extensive employment of armor and strong concrete works, stronger obstacles, as well as being supplied with armored artillery.

Such permanent localities and lines cannot be taken with the usual means of field operations; these latter may suffice, however, when the defenses are either obsolete or sparsely defended.

In most cases, the attacker confines himself in the beginning to driving back the hostile advanced troops and preventing the fortress or fortified lines from operating outside their confines, so that they can no longer effect the movements of the field army. In the case of a fortress, the general situation determines whether the fortress is to be completely invested or whether it is sufficient to cripple the fortress at a certain sector on the front.

For the execution of an attack against modern fortifications, orders therefor are awaited from general headquarters. The latter also furnishes the special means for the attack.

It should be thoroughly considered whether it is necessary to chain down the available strongest means of attack and material portions of the field army against strong fortifications and weaker forces of the enemy.

358. In attacking permanent fortifications, there are different methods of attack, from among which, the most suitable one in each instance is selected.

ms

Surprise leads to success quickest, that is, surprise without artillery preparation..

Next to surprise attack comes the attack in force, aided by the employment of an enormous mass of artillery. The infantry sharply attacks the enemy and shaking his morale so badly in such a short time that he believes his cause to be lost.

The bombardment is purely an artillery attack, which leads to the objective when principally employed against smaller places or against forts surrounding populous cities.

Under certain conditions and when artillery is lacking, investment is the only means for taking a fortress. Capitulation is forces by hunger.

The planned attack requires the largest expenditure of time and forced. It is considered only when all other attack methods preclude chances of success.

ms

# X. DEFENSE.

## A. GENERAL PRINCIPLES.

354. Defense intended to hold a position and defeat any attack against it and to decisively beat the enemy, is combined with offensive action.

Any position is of value, only when it forces the enemy to attack and, during the enemy's attempt at envelopment procures for the defender the necessary time or favorable conditions for his offensive action.

Proper arrangements are always made for rapid shifting of forces.

Each troop unit arranges for deep defense by groups. This specially applies to open situations.

Every position is immediately reinforced. False works and changes in the position made during the night are advantageous.

## B. DEFENSE IN OPEN SITUATIONS.

355. A fortified field position is a zone of resistance constructed with means available in the field. It seldom consists of continuous lines but generally consists of a system of fox holes, small nests for single arms (machine guns, rifle squads, trench mortars, field pieces) or larger strong points for the different arms, that are irregularly grouped and strongly organized in depth.

The depth of a position depends on the strength of the available troops, the width of the sectors assigned them, the battle objectives, and the terrain.

Camouflage is very important; it is arranged prior to the beginning of construction work.

356. The foremost edge of the position generally is the main line of resistance. It is the line in front of which, the enemy is broken by concentrated fire of all arms. It is retaken if the enemy succeeds in entering the position and must be in the hands of the troops at the completion of battle. Its location depends mainly on the location of the artillery observation stations. It is sufficiently far in front of them. Adapted to the terrain, frequently situated just behind a ridge, or leading straight through villages and woods, it is hidden as much as possible from the enemy's sight. In no case, should it be possible for the enemy to distinguish it as the line of main resistance. Protection against hostile tanks is striven for (water, swamp, rocky declivities).

The works are constructed so as to make difficult the hostile ground and aerial reconnaissance; for that reason and for the purpose of splitting up the hostile fire, rifle pits and nests are advanced beyond the strong points and the forces are not crowded together in the line of main resistance. All defense works mutually flank each other; this specially applies to machine guns.

/en

The trace of the main line of resistance is exactly known by the artillery so that it can regulate its fire accordingly.

If there is insufficient time for construction of numerous nests and strong points, some nests and points are constructed at the most important points of the position.

Placing outposts, organized in depth, far in front of the position is generally advisable. They, on the one hand, keep the enemy in doubt as to the location of the main line of resistance and on the other permit a sufficient insight into the attack terrain of the enemy, which frequently is unobtainable from the main line of resistance. Frequent change of location of these posts is advantageous to protect them against operations of hostile patrols, and to leave the enemy uncertain as to the distribution of our resistance.

Whether these outposts fall back on the main forces prior to the hostile attack, or whether they offer stubborn resistance, depends on the entire situation and is made known to the troops when they take up those positions. A change in procedure may become necessary during the course of the battle.

Success is always sought, in fighting for possession of the main line of resistance. After an attack is repulsed, outposts are again sent out.

The commander of the troops supervises the conduct of the outposts in front of the different sectors so that it will be harmonious.

The outposts, on their part, secure information of conditions with the enemy by frequent raids. They keep the foreground up to the enemy's lines in their possession.

Artillery is placed to support these outposts.

358. A position is seldom found that is excellent in all respects, especially in an extensive position. The shortcomings of any position are offset by correct distribution of forces, by full use of all flanking possibilities in our own sector and between neighboring sectors, establishment of nests and strong points under cover, construction of numerous bombproofs and numerous weakly occupied false works, and by construction of masks and pitfalls. The garrison in front, and also all units farther in rear are located so they are able to participate by direct and indirect fire at long and mid range in the defeat of the hostile attack. Commanding positions for the heavy machine guns are selected.

The principal requirements are: extensive and protected ground observation for the artillery, sufficient field of fire for the infantry, and good covered communication between all important portions of the position.

At the same time defensive works are constructed, obstacles are constructed and ranges measured to points in the foreground. In case of need, roads and bridges are constructed, and prominent objects that might facilitate the enemy's bombardment are removed.

Complete information is obtained as to the most important routes of approach for the enemy and of his places for assembly. These places are swept by an effective artillery fire.

/en

The railroads leading to the position and the probable detraining stations of the enemy are observed continuously. Those, not within the zone of effective artillery fire, especially the detraining stations, are harassed by aerial forces.

Frequently the garrison of nests and strong points defend themselves in front or to one side of their works, and to accomplish this, they even seek the open terrain when the hits of the hostile artillery make such procedure advisable. This method, however, is used only under direct orders from platoon and higher commanders. Even the smallest garrison is instructed what to do in case of alarm and hostile attack.

259. It may be advantageous to have in front of the main position, advanced positions, temporarily occupied. These are for the purpose of; preventing the attacker from prematurely capturing prominent and dominating points in the foreground, inducing him to deploy in a wrong direction, and increasing his difficulties in working up to the main position.

Defense of these advanced positions is executed by very weak infantry detachments or dismounted cavalry with numerous machine guns, and by heavy and light artillery firing on a broad front and from positions that are difficult to perceive. This is done to deceive the enemy.

Timely withdrawal is always considered, as otherwise there is danger of the enemy following up these advanced troops and reaching the main position with them. The main position supports advanced positions only by artillery fire.

360. In the matter of posting the artillery in the main position, the selection of good ground observation stations is more important than the firing positions themselves. A clear view into the battle terrain of the infantry, in rear of our own most advanced line, as well as far in rear of the hostile front is necessary. A view into the terrain of the probable hostile battery positions is very desirable, but hardly possible except in very exceptional cases. Observation at short ranges is best, when a view of the hostile position is obtained from a dominating hill far in rear or in the flank. In other cases, single portions of the main line of resistance are bent farther forward to protect the observation.

The batteries, protected by machine guns, are posted so that the majority of them are able to direct their fire on the attacking enemy even when the advanced observation fails and observation is made from points in rear. The batteries are posted in great depth. This has the advantage of splitting up the hostile fire and of keeping strong portions of the artillery fit for action up to the moment of the assault, even under very difficult conditions.

It is also advantageous to place single field pieces or platoons in well constructed positions far in front to serve as special defense in the assault; these are kept absolutely concealed until the very last moment, and then take the assaulting enemy by surprise with direct fire- this fire is specially directed on the enemy's tanks. Batteries of the short range artillery are used for this purpose and the infantry batteries are kept mobile as a general rule.

/en

361. The commander divides the position into sectors, which he assigns to the separate units for fortification and occupation.

The width of these sectors depends on the nature of the terrain. In a terrain that is easy to defend, the width is relatively large; few troops but plenty of ammunition is required. On the other hand, where, because of a covered field of fire and the fact that the defender has insufficient artillery, the enemy is able to get close to the position under cover, the sectors are made very narrow and are more strongly occupied.

362. By well planned fortifications and by correct distribution of troops, the commander of the troops is able to use a small number of men in the front, while he makes his reserve as strong as possible. Artillery and tanks are attached to the reserve.

363. The formation in depth, which is absolutely required within the different sectors, is limited by the principle, that the most important requirement is to break the enemy's assault in front of the position by the fire of all arms. Therefore, a sufficient defense against assault is provided.

Portions of the enemy that enter the position, and cannot be dealt with by flanking fire, by local counter attack, nests, and strong points, are immediately driven out by a counter attack of the reserves held in readiness for that purpose. Warning is given against splitting up reserves when they are used.

364. The reserve is placed in readiness at a point from where it can start for the prepared counter attack, depending on the direction of the hostile main attack and the terrain. Employment of railroads and motor trucks for shifting the reserves may have to be considered.

In case the position is not protected on both flanks, the reserves are posted generally in rear of one of the unprotected flanks.

When the reserve is echeloned with the intention of striking the enemy's flank, the counter attack is ordered when it appears that the hostile main force is engaged in the frontal attack.

365. The artillery opens fire in accordance with orders from the commander of the troops, as soon as there is no longer any necessity for the artillery to remain in hiding, and when paying targets present themselves. Interdiction fire, annihilation fire, and destructive fire are used to increase the difficulties of the hostile approach, to prevent the enemy from taking up a position in readiness for attack, from bringing up supplies, and for annihilating his offensive works.

The carefully controlled artillery fire is specially directed against the deploying hostile artillery: full use being made of aerial observation and the flash and sound ranging sections. The artillery fire is kept on the hostile batteries only, until the hostile infantry goes into position of readiness for the assault and starts the assault. As soon as this is perceived, the majority of the batteries direct their fire on the hostile infantry, and the remainder of the batteries continue to fire on the hostile artillery. Our own infantry now also opens fire on the hostile infantry with its heavy guns. The light machine guns are the principal defensive arms in the assault.

/en

The enemy is confronted with new tasks again and again, by sudden changes in the location of the defensive groups.

Broad gaps, caused by casualties, are perceived by the highest commander in good time and closed by sending in reserves.

366. The defender does not proceed to a counter attack from the position until he has defeated the assault and exhausted the effect of his fire arms, or unless it is a question of driving off an enemy who has broken down under fire in front of the position. Great success is accomplished in this way. A premature counter attack may lead to fatal reverses and to the loss of the position.

367. All arms make the necessary preparations in daytime for firing at night and for meeting a night attack.

Every hostile approach is timely perceived and all chances for surprise precluded by increased patrol service and listening posts, by sending out intelligence squads, and by illuminating the foreground.

Support of the attacked infantry by artillery is assured at all times, even at night. In case of a night attack, the sector reserves fall in without waiting for orders, and expel with cold steel, any enemy that has entered the position. In night attacks, the reserve under orders of the commander of the troops, is placed in readiness for maching.

## C. DEFENSE IN STABILIZED SITUATIONS.

368. Permanent positions are defensive positions during a long period when operations are at a standstill, as may occur at the conclusion of open warfare or fighting for a position that has not resulted in a decision.

The locations are selected so that they are suited not only for defense, but also offer good exit points for a subsequent attack. It is sometimes necessary to create these requisites by an attack with a limited objective or by moving back the front.

369. These positions are generally constructed in the shape of fortified field positions. It is of special importance to locate the position of the outposts, the main line of resistance, and the position itself in long drawn out stabilized situations with the stronger fighting means. Defense for all assaults is accomplished by the construction of numerous and strong obstacles (even wire obstacles charged with electricity), establishment of observation stations, machine gun, trench mortar and searchlight positions. By continually strengthening the position, especially constructing numerous strong points, by assured and secure wire communication, by placing single field pieces in strong and covered positions far to the front, and by keeping field pieces and platoons of artillery always in readiness with trains hitched up, stubborn resistance is made possible, even against hostile tanks, and captured portions of the position can soon be retaken.

The greatest value is attached to having all works hidden from the enemy especially from his aerial observation. This is specially true for combat stations, bombproofs, observation stations, machine gun nests, trench mortar stations, battery positions and ammunition dumps.

370. The first endeavor is to create a first line position. Traffic between the different nests and strong points, reserves and bombproofs, demands communicating trenches, in the subsequent enlargement of the position.

/en

The trace of these communicating trenches must, however, offer no clear picture to the hostile aerial reconnaissance, nor to artillery observers of the distribution of our troops, and are, therefore, constructed irregularly and with plenty of false and misleading works. They do not avoid detours.

This results in the position showing irregular trunk trenches located in rear of each other, into which approach trenches lead from the rear.

It is endeavored to arrange the trenches so that each trench can support the trench in its front to defeat a hostile assault. The distance between trenches is about 200 meters on the average. This distance is increased or decreased, depending on the terrain and in consideration of the effective depth of the hostile artillery fire.

Communication and approach trenches are prepared for defense and offer facilities for delivering flank fire.

371. Construction of observation stations for infantry and artillery is of special importance. They are located at a certain distance in rear of the line of main resistance, and are provided with visual signal means for communication with troops and command posts.

372. Bombproofs are for the purpose of keeping the garrison and the reserves in good fighting condition up to the moment of the assault. They are irregularly located in nests and strong points and also in rear of them and on the flanks. As a general rule extensive bombproofs are not constructed in the foremost portions of the position. They prevent the rapid exit of the garrison. In front, smaller works of the simplest kind suffice. When time and conditions permit, they are constructed of concrete and steel. Number and size of bombproofs increase with increase of distance from the enemy.

373. Command posts are constructed as strong as possible and so arranged that the leader is able to insert his will on his troops. A clear view and proximity to the reserve is desirable. Avoid placing command posts near prominent points in the terrain. Possibility of good communications must obtain (specially wire, wireless communication.)

374. Artillery positions are selected in similar manner as in defense of fortified field positions. Ranges are measured. Arrangements are made for change of positions and for employment of reinforcing batteries; in this relation, construction of command posts and observation stations or observation centers with proper communications is most important.

Arrangements for the work of artillery flash and sound ranging sections are made along the entire front.

Panoramic sketches, aerial photos, and artillery maps are started in good time.

375. Greatest attention is paid to storing ammunition, to construction of obstacles, transmission of information, and unceasing care for the comfort of the troops.

/en

Communications to the rear are improved and constantly kept in good condition. Water supply is regulated.

376. Besides enlargement of the first position, construction of positions farther in rear is soon started. These latter serve principally for mobile battlefield defense. Only the highest commander issues orders for occupying a position in rear or portions thereof.

377. Distances between positions in rear and the front line position and between themselves are arranged so that after the foremost position is pierced it is necessary for the hostile artillery to deploy again before attacking the rear position. The distance between positions in rear is at least 5 kilometers The terrain sometimes compels exceptions to this general rule.

378. Switch positions, running diagonally, are of advantage where specially endangered portions of the front demand, a successful entry on the part of the enemy be contained.

379. As a general rule, the enlargement of the primary position is performed by the fighting troops that occupy the respective sector; construction and enlargement of rear positions is performed by labor battalions.

## OCCUPATION OF POSITIONS AND PREPARATIONS AGAINST HOSTILE ATTACK.

380. Infantry units are employed side by side, and in smaller commands, they are also strongly formed in depth; employment of machine guns, trench mortars, grenade throwers, etc., saves men.

In quiet periods, portions of the infantry are quartered in villages and camps in rear of the position. But their timely return to the position, when the situation demands, is ordered, even when a hostile attack on a larger scale is only expected but has not yet been perceived with full assurance. Considerations for the comfort of troops in this case are ignored, and the entire infantry of the sector is kept in full battle readiness.

Preparations are made for use of railroads and motor trucks to bring up the infantry for tactical employment.

The commander of the troops calculates for all his movements and measures, on a greater use of time and forces, in a terrain covered with gas than in terrain free of gas. The matter of gas has a material influence on bringing up the reserves and timely regulation of employment of troops.

381. The infantry commanders of all ranks distribute the sector assigned them among their troops, and take proper measures to maintain their influence on the course of events by holding out a proper reserve. It is well to divide the troops into combat troops, supports, and reserves.

Reliefs are not made too frequently. The commander to be relieved, generally regulates the matter of relief and relinguishes command only when actually relieved.

382. Every man knows what point he is to hold. Offensive conduct of smaller detachments is permissible only when it will not lead to the loss of their own position in case of non-success.

/en

It is the duty of all commanders to personally supervise all measures taken. They convince themselves by frequent tests on the terrain, that cooperation is assured in battle by all portions of the command.

The lower infantry and artillery commanders, being familiar with each others positions and observation stations, regulate their co-operation accordingly. They are quartered as close together as is permissible in consideration of assured communication with the troops under their command.

When it is impracticable to quarter in the same place, the infantry and artillery commanders, working together in one sector, artillery liaison officers are attached to infantry battalion headquarters.

383. The infantry commanders are responsible for continuous close reconnaissance. This reconnaissance ascertains the exact situation with the enemy as well as with our own troops. Proper arrangements are made for rapid transmission of results to the rear.

The higher leader supplements the close reconnaissance by watching the hostile communications and by employing infantry and artillery airplanes.

384. In transition to stabilized situations, the artillery requires a new organization of command conditions, and requires increased echelonment in depth. It is thereby better able to take advantage of its possibility of producing effect, and can offer more resistance in the defense. Its fighting power is also conserved for a longer time.

The artillery is under the orders of the division commander; still, corps headquarters may retain artillery and long-range flat trajectory artillery that is charged with special tasks.

385. The division commander assigns the missions of the artillery to the division artillery commander. The latter then conducts the artillery fight and is in charge of the entire artillery attached to the division, except the infantry batteries. The division artillery is divided into groups, which in turn divide themselves into sub-groups.

It is advisable to designate definite short range battle groups or sub-groups for the different infantry sectors, with which they remain in continuous communication, and which they always support. When the sectors are very broad and the terrain close, a portion of the short range batteries, in addition to infantry batteries, are placed under the orders of the infantry commanders. But this procedure is the exception in stabilized situations.

Long range fighting groups are formed as a general rule to fire on the hostile artillery and distant targets. When the artillery is weak, such groupings are not made.

Employing the means placed at his disposal by the division, the artillery commander of the division arranges for communication with the groups under his orders, for communication between these groups, and for extension of special artillery communications (Flash and sound ranging systems.)

/en

386. In accordance with the instructions received from the division commander, the division artillery commander draws up an artillery battle plan. He independently arranges for offensive employment of artillery and for direct protection of the infantry. He distributes the missions among the groups and supervises their execution. He regulates the cooperation between artillery and the other arms and makes agreement with the artillery of neighboring sectors for mutual support. He is responsible for expenditures and replenishment of artillery ammunition.

387. The main point is to provide the most effective fire protection for the infantry as soon as possible, in each and every battle situation.

Placing the batteries designated, to secure that protection too close to the line of main resistance, is an error. These important batteries would be silenced too early. Beyond this, no hard and fast rules can be laid down for posting the artillery, that matter depends principally on the terrain.

388. Preparations for repulsing a hostile attack are made so that, when the infantry demands it at latest, or on signals from the artillery airplanes (light signals, wireless, etc) the artillery can lay down annihilation fire. This fire is delivered shock-like and in rapid sequence and soon changes into slower fire. It is delivered on, and in the immediate front of, hostile trenches, bombproofs, approach trenches, and on the terrain in rear of the position, and every place where the assault infantry and tanks are supposed to be or seen to be assembling or approaching. Delivering annihilation fire along the entire front is effective and necessary, only in very exceptional cases. It leads to unnecessary dispersion of fire.

Timely and correct employment of observation airplanes materially assists in perceiving the hostile infantry attack in its position in readiness. The hostile infantry can then be held down by fire, and can be fired on with annihilation fire before it starts the assault.

Fire protection by artillery and trench mortars at night is called for by special light signals. These light signals are regulated by the commander of the troops and are charged from time to time, so that the enemy cannot employ them to our disadvantage. The signals sent up from the front line are transmitted to the artillery by relays. When communication with the front fails during heavy infantry and machine gun fire, the artillery uses its independent judgment about fire protection in any sector.

In case of fog, special measures (accustic signals) are required for calling for fire protection.

When in spite of the annihilation fire, the enemy succeeds in leaving his trenches for the assault, the artillery fire is changed into barrage fire and withdrawn to immediately in front of our infantry. Because of dispersion, a few shots sometimes fall short, endangering our own infantry. Barrage fire is started by the artillery independently.

The balloon is specially suited for observing barrage and annihilation fire.

The infantry must never expect that the barrage and annihilation fire alone will defeat the hostile attack. It merely remains a material support of infantry. The infantry defeats the hostile assault with its own heavy and light arms.

/en

389. In urgent cases, additional batteries are brought up to participate in annihilation and barrage fire. They fire over the regular batteries which generally employ flat trajectory fire. Later on these batteries resume their previous fire.

390. In addition, all trench mortars are employed as a general rule, to reinforce the annihilation and barrage fire. The division artillery commander regulates this matter.

391. The batteries that are not required for the fire protection solve the usual tasks of the artillery. They damage the enemy continually, particularly his artillery.

The most effective fire that can be thrown on the hostile artillery is destructive fire, delivered by the heavy and medium calibers and also by the light batteries (long range artillery), which are placed a material distance in front of the batteries charged with fire protection. This decreases the hostile fighting power and facilitates the fighting of our infantry. The fire is directed on observation stations, ammunition dumps, equipment and crews. Success depends on well observed, carefully controlled, and surprise fire (airplane, balloon, flash and sound ranging sections, ground observation). Counter-battery work at the time of hostile attack preparation, is the principal task of the long range artillery. This is not neglected even after the hostile attack has started. Timely resort to gas shells is of great effect.

All the hostile trenches cannot be destroyed. Besides destroying the enemy's artillery, important works and accessories such as, trench mortars in well prepared positions, machine guns, bombproofs, etc., are destroyed.

392. Interdiction and harassing fire is constantly employed in stabilized situations and is fully prepared to defeat the hostile attack. It is delivered against all kinds of hostile traffic, against headquarters, shelters, parks, railroad stations, etc. All kinds of guns, especially long range guns, participate in that kind of fire. The farther it reaches into the terrain in rear, the more it disturbs the enemy. Delivered in surprise, it can cause material loss to the enemy. At night it is of special value, having a great moral effect. Employment of gas shells also gives good results.

393. As a general rule, batteries are held mobile for engaging hostile artillery, and for delivering interdiction and harassing fire, and they change positions frequently. The resulting discomfort is borne by the batteries. At night, platoons or pieces near the front infantry line fire from positions not prepared in advance, but from which the ranges have been measured. They change their location again immediately after firing.

394. Hostile tanks are engaged by all the artillery in conjunction with machine guns and trench mortars with good expectation of rapid and thorough success. Endeavor is always made to reconnoiter and to annihilate the tanks in their waiting and starting positions. If there are good reasons to assume that they are approaching, then interdiction fire is principally delivered on the routes of approach, roads, folds and depressions in the terrain.

When a tank attack starts, the batteries that have been brought forward to engage the hostile artillery or to deliver harassing fire, deliver their fire on the approaching tanks instead; later on the batteries designated for the infantry fire protection also participate. Tanks that push their

/en

way forward in spite of this fire are destroyed by the fire of short range guns in prepared positions by direct fire at short range. Finally, every battery in position farther in rear is quickly prepared to fight tanks that are entering the position.

In most instances, it is advisable to hold out special reserves for engaging tanks only. These reserves generally consist of trench mortars, machine guns with armor piercing and explosive ammunition, and above all, field guns. These mobile reserves, either drawn by teams or carried on motor trucks, move to meet the tanks. Excellent wire communication is required in this matter.

395. Attaching platoons of horse artillery to the infantry, in addition to the infantry batteries is often advisable. Like the infantry batteries, they serve to support the infantry against a penetration, and especially to accompany a counter attack. Rapid employment is necessary. These platoons do not participate in other missions of artillery.

396. In stabilized situations, the higher commanders hold out artillery reserves, to employ them at points where the enemy is preparing or executing an attack.

397. Supporting artillery in positions in rear is always of advantage, as it offers a rallying place in case of a reverse, and when necessary, forms the skeleton of a new artillery concentration in position. However, single portions of the artillery in position is never drawn back for that purpose.

398. By means of uninterrupted and careful reconnaissance, the hostile attack intentions are perceived in good time. When extensive preparations indicate the probability of an attack on a large scale, the commander of the troops decides whether to accept the attack in the selected position or whether to fall back to a more favorable position.

399. When the commander decides to accept the attack, then the defensive front is at once prepared for the main battle. The following enumerated preparations, that have been made during the course of the quiet stabilized situation and should now be completed, are of special importance, viz:

Calculation and assembly of the necessary troops, ammunition, subsistence, equipment and supplies of all kinds;

Increase in number of command posts. When reenforcements are excepted, the new division and regimental boundary lines can seldom be designated in advance;

Preparation of observation stations and reinforcements positions for the artillery;

Extension of means of communication to the rear. Extension of the existing railroad net and arrangements made for large troop movements and increased forward movement of supplies. Extension to field railroads and tramways.

Protection of the communications to the rear against hostile aerial attacks and interference by inhabitants.

Improvement and enlargement of airdromes, of the aerial information net and anti-aircraft defense.

/en

Reconnaissance and establishment of places to anchor captive balloons.

Increase of signaling and communication means.

Extension of shelters and water supply.

Placing construction materials in readiness and arranging for additional labor forces.

Replenishment of ammunition dumps and engineer parks, establishment of an implement and tool reserve, establishment of work and repair shops, construction gas depots for the necessary supply for balloons.

Enlargement of the supply of maps.

Removal of inhabitants.

400. Carefully watching the hostile positions and the terrain in rear by continually taking aerial photos thereof, gives by comparison, the best means for determining the enemy's intentions.

When this phase of aerial reconnaissance can no longer be regularly carried on and without showing gaps because of the hostile resistance, the aerial pursuit units are materially reinforced. Their attack clears the road for the observation units and particularly holds down the hostile artillery and combat airplanes. Concentrated and protracted bombing attacks against a few important objectives, such as hostile detraining stations, airdromes, ammunition dumps, and depots, materially delays and interrupts the hostile preparations. Aerial attack is carried on during the night against the routes of approach and shelters of the enemy.

401. The reconnaissance activity of the intelligence troops is important. The results thereof, enable the commander of the troops to at once perceive the main direction of the enemy's attack. In order to increase this reconnaissance activity, all methods of communication that interfere with listening in on the hostile traffic are for the time being, abandoned.

402. The divisions, designated for holding the first position, are timely placed; the divisions not required therefor at the beginning, take position as reserves (counter attack divisions) in rear of the front line.

In addition, the artillery is reinforced and the power of resistance of all positions increased with all means at hand. Questions of command, are clearly defined. At the time of the hostile attack, everything is in complete readiness down to the last detail.

403. By increasing the mobility of outposts, the difficulties of the hostile reconnaissance are increased.

## EXECUTION OF THE DEFENSE

404. The defense always counts on a surprise attack by the enemy. If that takes place, the divisions in front hold their assigned positions even against great numerical superiority. There, they break the first rush of the hostile attack, cripple his power of attack, and give the commander of the troops the necessary time to bring up reserves and execute other counter measures. When the frontal defense is strong, it is possible to obtain a complete success.

/en

405. When the approaching attack is timely perceived, the mass of the artillery and trench mortars fire on the hostile exit points and places of assembly. Thereby the hostile infantry attack is crushed in its incipient stages by our massed fire.

Counter battery work and firing on the hostile routes of approach, shelters and communications to the rear, commences as early as possible. A well planned gas bombardment on a large scale can materially hinder the enemy's preparations.

During the progress of the battle, full use is made of mobile defense and the deep echelonment of the artillery. In case of a hostile penetration, only the batteries in front suffer. The hostile assault breaks on the batteries in rear. Always keep in mind a renewed formation in depth, and never lose sight of the situation of the infantry.

406. The infantry defends itself with the fire of all its arms. Mutual support of the different strong points by fire, and, at favorable moments by rapid counter attacks is of decisive importance. Annihilating and barrage fire of the artillery and trench mortars are repeatedly used to keep off the following attack waves of the enemy.

Detachments in rear are held in readiness for the counter attack and are started at once if the enemy enters the position.

When the position is evacuated at some points by orders,provisions are made to pass over to the attack and regain those lost portions.

407. When local counter attacks are unsuccessful in driving the enemy out of the position, then a systematic counter attack is started.

Counter attacks, especially in force, require detailed preparations. Detailed orders are issued for position in readiness, time, target, battle sector of zone of action, artillery and trench mortar preparations, participation of airplanes and tanks. Overhasty action generally leads to defeat. On the other hand, every unnecessary delay gives the enemy increased advantage and assists him to gain a firm foothold in the captured terrain.

Counter attacks are frequently directed against the flanks of the enemy who has penetrated the position.

408. Counter attack divisions held in reserve are brought forward at the proper time.

It is always attempted to employ them as a whole. Only lack of sufficient counter attack divisions justifies their partial employment for support at several threatened points of the front. The parts detached in that case are under the orders of the respective division commanders in the front line.

It is necessary to keep motor truck columns or railroad trains in readiness at least for the dismounted troops.

409. When there are no counter attack divisions, the battle is conducted so that the entire defensive sector cannot be pierced, and so that the hostile power of attack is broken by resistance in depth, and by the support of the different positions.

/on

Such a procedure demands great skill on the part of the commander of the troops. By constantly changing the formation and by maintaining liaison and working in cooperation with adjacent troops, he will skillfully give way at a point where confronted by superior numbers and will make a stubborn resistance at another point (mobile defense).

410. Advantage is taken of the mobile defense in cases where the troops suffice to hold the first position, but where the commander of the troops has confidence in his troops, he desires to finish the defense with an attack.

An attack on our part is always attempted after the defeat of a hostile assault, in the face of a shaken enemy, and when there still are sufficient forces.

411. Should the defender gradually lose ground in spite of stubborn resistance and employment of all fighting means against a superior enemy, and is forced back into unprepared terrain, then, the resistance is continued there by mobile defense. Previous selection of new positions is required for this. The method of battle approaches that in open situations, supported by the stronger means used in stabilized situations. The terrain is fortified at once.

412. Endeavor is made to relieve the divisions in front during a long continued battle. The general rule is to relieve by entire divisions. When there are no complete divisions, then regiments in the front line that have suffered most are sometimes relieved by corresponding units taken from fronts that have not yet been attacked. Simultaneous relief of infantry and artillery leads to material interference in the battle activity. On the other hand, a long separation of the artillery from its proper division is very undesirable and is avoided.

The tanks, engineers, information, wireless and airplane units fighting in the most advanced line are also timely relieved.

## D. DEFENSE

### PERMANENT FORTIFICATIONS

413. The defender of permanent fortifications, insofar as his forces permit, draws a strong enemy onto himself by offensive action and thereby supports the field armies fighting in his vicinity. Thus, he most effectively compels the enemy to pay attention to the fortress or fortified line.

Fortifications, situated outside the zone of operations of the field armies, also contain strong forces of the enemy. This frequently is accomplished by offensive operations with the mobile portions of the fortress but in which case, care is exercised that these portions are not cut off from the fortress. If the enemy then turns against the fortress, it is defended to the utmost. Even the mere possession of the locality may be of importance. The main point is, always to husband our forces and to chain down as many hostile troops as possible.

The defender offers protracted and stubborn resistance in a position in front of the fortress if the terrain favors this procedure, or if the selected position is so close to the fortress that it can be materially supported by the latter, especially by its artillery. In this case also, attention is paid to keeping open the route of retreat and to maintaining constant communication with the fortress.

It is the task of the defender to get along in most cases with weak forces. Only then is the object of the fortress attained. The details of carrying on a battle are similar to those of any defense.

/en

## XI. ENGAGEMENTS UNDER SPECIAL CONDITIONS

### A. DELAYING ACTION

414. The commander of the troops carries out his intention to engage in a delaying action on a broad front, by the manner of utilizing his forces. The special battle purpose is not necessarily divulged to the troops, The troops carry on any attack with full decision and, in defense, hold the position by using the very last force available.

Employment of strong aerial forces and increased employment of balloons is materially instrumental in deceiving the enemy as to the intentions of the commander of the troops. Much work is done with the spade.

415. The best way to delay the decision is attained by deploying a strong and mobile artillery at long ranges. Premature opening of fire holds the attention of the enemy in attack, and, in defense, causes his deployment. Increased expenditure of ammunition is necessary.

416. Infantry is employed sparingly; strong reserves are held out. The reserves are not used unless the purpose of the battle changes.

417. Deceiving engagements are for the purpose of misleading the enemy and for causing him to take wrong measures. Generally they have no supports and are effective only when the enemy believes the battle serious in consideration of terrain and general situation.

Even if special measures are taken against hostile aerial reconnaissance, it is difficult, when the terrain is open, to deceive the enemy for any length of time.

### B. VILLAGE AND FOREST FIGHTING.

418. Villages are natural supporting points. They not only offer protection against sight from the ground and increase the difficulties of aerial observation, but because of their massive construction also offer protection against infantry fire, the fire of light and medium artillery, and light trench mortars. Their importance increases with their size. But nevertheless we avoid turning them into local points of the battle, as in their interior the forces are soon consumed and frequently without having gained any influence on the decision.

419. When approaching the enemy, the attacker seldom leads his force through villages. These places almost always are under artillery fire. And in the attack, it is best for the attacker to advance his main force on one side of a village occupied by the enemy. He attempts to hold down the village by fire and to take it from the flank or rear. Special units are designated for that attack before the start is made. Attaching armored automobiles and tanks are advisable. The attackers main force continues the advance in the original direction.

420. When the infantry has worked up close to the village, the

ms

artillery shifts its fire towards the enemy. At the same time, the infantry pushes into the village and opens a road for itself to the other edge of it with cold steel, hand grenades, trench mortars and flame throwers.

Frequently, when opposed by a tenacious enemy, the attacker is able to advance only step by step, in which procedure, the houses and outbuildings are made ready for assault by artillery and trench mortars. After capture of the village, no part thereof is left unsearched. Crowding the foremost lines is avoided, strong reserves are held out to guard against reverses.

421. The defender generally draws villages into his position, but as they attract the hostile artillery fire, he occupies them in force only when the location is favorable and when they are of massive construction.

422. In most cases the main line of resistance does not run through the edge of a village. It runs in front of the village or leads square through the village. Reinforcing works are specially valuable. Obstacles and blockades, especially against tanks, increase the difficulties of the approach of the enemy to the edge of the village and assure good defense within the place. Projecting houses, gardens, hedges, are used for sweeping the edge of the village, the streets and the obstacles. Precautions are taken against gas.

423. When the defender locates his center of gravity in the village, he runs danger of being cut off by the enemy advancing on both sides of the village. Therefore very strong reserves are placed outside the village under complete cover. These attack the enemy from the flank. The village garrison drives out the enemy that has entered the village with cold steel. When this is not successful, then every building and every sector is defended stubbornly. The subordinate commanders here find a good field of activity.

424. Woods offer protection against sight and observation from the air, but when foliage is absent woods offer little protection from aerial view. Fire effect against larger woods, especially woods consisting of tall trees with dense underbrush, is materially weakened. But woods are specially exposed to the danger of gas. Attacking through woods is specially difficult; the defender on the other hand can hold out against even superior forces.

Maintenance of communication within extensive woods encounters serious obstacles. Roads and trails facilitate finding the way and frequently, in dense woods, offer the only chance for the movement of troops. We avoid splitting up our forces. The commander keeps his troops well in hand; this can be done without trouble considering the diminished hostile fire effect.

425. The attacker attempts to take possession of smaller woods by envelopment and by gassing them. This method attains the object more quickly and more surely than a direct attack. Flank fire from the woods is prevented by our own artillery fire.

ms

When it is necessary for the attacker to directly attack the wood, he principally turns against projecting portions thereof, which have previously been bombarded by artillery and trench mortars.

After the forest is entered, order is at once established and the troops are organized anew. The troops then continue the advance in skirmish squads and light machine gun squads followed by dense skirmish lines, which are in turn followed by supports in close order; echeloned reserves with machine guns protect the flanks. Flame throwers are specially effective as the smoke clouds remain long and have a crippling effect on the enemy. Trench mortars, infantry batteries, and other portions of the short range artillery placed under the orders of the infantry commanders, support the infantry while the artillery of the division brings support only after a more protracted time, and after the situation has been thoroughly cleared.

Where the woods are not too deep, the penetration continues to the opposite edge.

426. The defender avoids the edge of the woods, because the edge offers a specially favorable target for the hostile artillery. He either enters the woods so far as he can still fire therefrom, or takes his position square through the woods or in front of the edge. The defense of a main line of resistance assuring cohesion is in most cases advantageous and even necessary when the density of the underbrush increases the difficulties of view. By skilful placing of the lines the actual location of the position is made difficult to perceive. Advanced positions with light machine guns at crossroads and clearings and even in trees are sometimes useful.

High angle fire artillery and trench mortars can fire within a forest after very minor preparations. Flat trajectory guns are posted at the rear edge of clearings and outside the woods.

If the attacker succeeds in entering the woods, then the defender drives him out again by attacks, especially against his flanks.

Extensive use is made of flanking machine guns, light trench mortars, and field pieces.

Blockades, by cutting down trees and regular obstacles, prevent the enemy from spreading out within the woods, and flame throwers and machine gun nests even located in trees, increase the difficulties of his advance.

Like fighting in villages, the forest fighting demands independent action in an increased degree on the part of all subordinate commanders and individuals. Superiority in numbers is of less importance than the bravery of the individual in hand to hand fighting.

## C. FIGHTING IN DARKNESS AND FOG.

427. Night attacks may be necessary to surprise the enemy and when we are inferior in airplanes and tanks. In addition, they are carried on in order to gain favorable positions from which to start a battle, to increase the success so far attained in battle, for the purpose of pursuit, as well as for screening the retreat.

mj

Night attacks frequently are indications of a decisive leadership, which, without fearing the difficulties connected therewith, only strives to maintain freedom of action and to finish an action with all means at hand without delay. But detailed reconnaissances by day and night, and getting the troops accustomed to the terrain, are absolutely required.

428. The commander, who orders a night attack, designates the hour and the objective according to the situation and condition of his troops. Whenever possible, fresh troops are employed.

429. Night attacks are frequently started during the early hours of the night. The intentions of the enemy are thereby crossed and his artillery defense materially damaged. The hostile commander of the troops is confronted with heavy decisions.

On the other hand, when the attack is started early in the night, the immediate exploitation of the vidtory is difficult. For that reason offensive operations on a larger scale are not started till daybreak. Darkness in that case is used only for going into position in readiness. This does not prevent the preparation for the main attack by minor attacks during the night, nor deceiving the enemy as to attack direction and time.

430. The difficulties of night attack increase with the strength of the command. Troops are used sparingly, especially in minor operations, because at night not the number but the moral value of the troops is decisive. Great success may be attained with minor means. But nevertheless the number used should correspond to the size of the tasks.

431. Infantry assumes the simplest formations at night. Smaller units mostly march in one column until close to the enemy. Then dense skirmish lines are formed or lines in close order with closely following up- supports and reserves, and the enemy is charged with cold steel either with or without fire preparation by artillery or trench mortars, according to the situation.

Larger units are formed into several assault columns. Plainly and exactly marking the routes of approach, places of going into readiness, and attack objectives and by timely regulation of the marches, readiness and start of the assault, it is endeavored to assure uniformity in the battle action. Care is taken to assure communication between columns, and after the hostile position has been entered, cohesion is established and assured. Plenty of time is given for all movements.

432. Artillery and trench mortars can prepare the infantry attack also at night. A short burst of fire generally suffices. In other cases, infantry attacks without artillery support and seeks success in surprise. The artillery always holds itself in readiness to immediately open fire against newly appearing hostile batteries, trench mortars, and against the enemy's routes of approach.

Suitable defensive means are placed in readiness to meet the attacks of the hostile attack airplanes that are certain to happen with the break of day.

ms

433. The best means of attaining success is surprise. Movements that are perceived by the enemy at dusk may betray the intention. Whether deceiving the enemy is possible through a false operation at some other point, remains to be considered; it may attract the attention of the enemy which it is desired to avoid.

Secrecy is also maintained as far as our own troops are concerned, until very shortly before the start of the attack. Reconnaissance is carried on without attracting attention, every noise of the marching troops is avoided.

It is best to plainly mark the direction of the attack on the terrain, and to hold reliable guides in readiness. Direction points are unobtrusively illuminated by searchlights in front of the troops. When the enemy uses searchlights from the ground or from the air, every movement immediately ceases and cover is sought by lying down. Obstacles that delay the march are timely removed. Comparison of watches is of great importance.

Darkness decreases the results of reconnaissance by airplanes and limits their participation in the battle on the ground. On the other hand, darkness favors bomb attacks from low altitudes against large targets.

434. Detailed instructions are given concerning the conduct after successful attacks and concerning assembly points in case of non-success.

435. Any defender, expecting a hostile attack, generally forms in denser groups at night.

Defense demands rest and circumspection on the part of every individual. Order and cohesion are specially necessary. Reserves are not used until the situation is clear. Illumination of the foreground protects against surprise.

436. Dense fog has the same influence on the battle activities as a clear night. General rules for conduct during fog are the same as in night fighting. But calculate at all times on the fact that the fog may rise or disperse. Therefore, any decision arrived at is executed as rapidly as possible.

Fog precludes employment of airplanes and balloon observation.

### D. FIGHTING FOR DEFILES AND STREAM CROSSINGS.

437. Defiles are principally an obstacle to movements. They interfere more with the attacker than with the defender. But they also hinder the latter if he desires to change from defense to attack.

Retrograde movements through a defile are specially difficult. Timely start of the march, strict leadership through the defile, and reception in rear of it by troops sent in advance, are necessary.

The pursuer generally strives for the annihilation of the enemy by rapidly pushing forward, mostly to one side, and by simultaneously blocking the defile.

ms

438. If both opponents are marching towards a defile with the intention of traversing it, that opponent who acts with greater celerity will have the advantage. Timely start and sending ahead mobile units with machine guns and artillery beyond the defile, as well as throwing artillery fire early on the terrain beyond the defile, is necessary.

439. Marching on a broad front is advantageous for opening several defiles simultaneously. In this manner, columns encountering difficulties in crossing are supported by other columns that have traversed their defile. But nevertheless, each column acts without loss of time in its place, as one column never knows whether its neighbors have encountered any difficulty and are awaiting support.

440. Waiting conduct in rear of a defile is proper only when the defile is not to be crossed for the time being, but only defended. Even then, reconnaissance extends beyond the defile.

Such a procedure is considered only, when it is certain that the enemy will cross the defile. A favorable chance for attack is created in that case. It is possible to materially damage the enemy and to open the defile at the time of the enemy's retreat by immediate and close pursuit.

441. When troops are forced to halt this side of the defile or within the defile, then the exit is secured as an invariable rule, by sending portions beyond the defile, unless it is not intended to continue the march.

In the defense of the defile, not only the slopes but also the bottom of the valley is occupied.

442. In many cases, it is impossible to ascertain the actual condition of a defile from the map. Therefore timely reconnaissance is necessary. The result can materially influence the battle conduct.

443. Streams and rivers form obstacles for the attacker but are, for the defender, a natural reinforcement of position. To both, they offer possibility of surprise by movements of troops.

444. The attacker gains a timely view of the terrain on the other side by ground and aerial reconnaissance, determines the most favorable crossing possibilities and, by taking quick possession of existing bridges and by gathering materials, takes all necessary measures that will facilitate rapid crossing. Hostile advanced detachments are driven to the other bank. Minor operations and deceiving operations are always carried on.

Defiles and river crossings are protected during the crossing by anti-aircraft guns and machine guns, against bombing, attack, and pursuit squadrons.

445. Those points where the river makes a bend are generally selected for the crossing. Uniform fire effect and flank protection for the portions that have crossed over the first is thereby gained.

ms

A covered approach towards the crossing is necessary, and in case of need, darkness is utilized. The portions that cross first establish a bridge head. They facilitate the crossing of the remaining portions, facilitate throwing of bridges and the crossing of the main body.

In selecting several points of crossing, select them so close together that success at one point means success at the next, and, on the other hand, so separated that the defender is forced to split up his forces.

446. In the face of the enemy, a crossing can succeed only by deploying strong covering troops, principally machine gun and artillery units. The hostile artillery covering the crossing is silenced and the stream defense, carried on by the hostile infantry, is broken.

All possible means are employed to deceive the enemy as to time and place of crossing.

After the leading infantry elements have successfully crossed, they require continuous support of our artillery until the troops that have crossed are strong enough to push forward. They push straight ahead into the hostile position. Debouchment up or down stream to support neighboring columns leads to flank attacks on the part of the enemy and lays our own crossing bare. Artillery is soon crossed over.

447. The defender increases the natural difficulties provided by the river by artificial means, and increases the power of defense and resistance by constructing positions at threatened points.

By advancing outposts or at least strong officers patrols beyond the stream, especially at favorable points for crossing, the approach of hostile scouts is prevented. By continuous reconnaissance, it is endeavored to timely learn the hostile measures. At night, the river is illuminated by searchlights.

448. The infantry occupies the river bank with sentries, which require special support near the probable crossing points.

In rear of them artillery takes specially favorable positions, which command the hostile routes of approach with long range flat trajectory fire, and from where they can throw a concentrated fire on the crossing points, and can also sweep the length of the river.

For the time being the mass of the troops is placed in readiness farther in rear. It falls in for attack as soon as the enemy is seen crossing. All mobile troops are attached to the main body of these troops. By attaching motor truck columns, and under certain conditions, railroad trains, assurance is had that these troops can be rapidly shifted. The reconnaissance and liaison troops attempt to ascertain as soon as possible the actual point of crossing.

Uncertainty of the situation easily leads to delay in starting the counter attack, and permits the enemy to establish bridgeheads. The danger of being deceived, on the other hand, requires caution on

ms

the part of the commander of the troops. Splitting up his forces is dangerous.

Employment of aerial attack squadrons against the enemy while crossing is always advantageous. Armed river steamers are very useful.

## E. MOUNTAIN FIGHTING.

449. Troops inured to mountains and properly equipped can overcome the difficulties and fatigues of mountain fighting. It is necessary for the commander to be familiar with the special combat requirements. He makes different calculations in regard to time and space than when fighting in lowlands.

450. Mountains confine the attacker to the passes. Road crossings become the focal points of fights. Advance along a broad front induces the defender to split up his forces and leaves him longer uncertain as to the main point of the attack.

But since the defender blockades the passes, it is necessary for the attacker to gain possession of the heights dominating these passes and to do this, he is forced to make extensive envelopments. For this purpose roads are not always available. Any envelopment demands considerable time and increases fatigue. But it has possibilities of large successes.

451. Lack of lateral communications increase the difficulties of mutual support and shifting of reserves. In this matter, the first onset of troops gains in importance in crossing mountains. The troop units fighting singly on the roads leading through passes, are not limited in their independence, and are made strong enough in the start to execute their tasks. They keep their reserves very close. When there is a suitable road net, motor truck columns facilitate a change in the distribution of forces and the shifting of reserves. In special cases, mainly at the edge of mountains, the question of using the railroad comes into consideration.

The difficulties of establishing wire communication is met by the employment of more wireless units.

452. Impossibility of getting a clear view of the terrain, frequent fog and snow, favor surprise in the conduct of battle. Weak, intrepid detachments gain advantages herein, while the very best defensive measures may become valueless. Dead angles are utilized.

Prior to any attack the terrain is thoroughly reconnoitered.

453. In the attack, mountain troops are employed at difficult places, on ridges, slopes, and in cut up terrain, while the other troops advance on roads. Artillery is always attached to the advance guard.

The attacker makes extensive use of flank fire, especially from dominating points. Trench mortars are specially suited to sweep dead angles.

ms

454. Mountain artillery can follow infantry even off the roads. Employment of artillery drawn by teams and motor trucks is confined to roads. The high angle fire of the howitzer makes that arm specially suited for mountain warfare; mortars also are a valuable arm in that respect in fights for passes or roads in the valleys. Long range guns are employed only to a limited extent.

Artillery preparation for opening fire, change of position, and ammunition supply requires a much longer time than in the lowlands. This is specially true in regard to the mountain artillery in action at great distances from the roads.

455. The defender principally blockades the roads leading through passes, occupies the heights dominating them and secures himself against envelopment. Because of the difficulties in shifting troops, the first formation and distribution of troops at his disposal is of increased importance. Motor truck columns and railroads are utilized as far as possible.

If the enemy succeeds in pushing across the mountains at some point, he is attacked in flank and rear by using all lateral communications and is driven back.

456. Passes are favorable targets for bombing attacks and are protected by anti-aircraft guns and machine guns.

457. Weather conditions play a far greater role in mountain warfare than in the lowlands. In absence of shelter in bad weather, the health of troops is much more affected. Heavy snow fall increases the difficulties of all movements. Intense cold makes great demands on the endurance of the attacker and defender. As the weather generally changes very suddenly in mountains, the decision, once arrived at, is rapidly executed, or its chances of being carried out diminish. Weather stations and inhabitants are frequently consulted concerning changes in the weather.

458. Bringing up supplies in mountains is difficult as railroads and the road net are as a rule scant and of little capacity. Difficulties in construction of field railroads are overcome to a very small extent by constructing cable roads.

459. Intermediate mountains generally offer little difficulty to infantry, while on the other hand, bringing up artillery and supplies is done with difficulty and loss of time. Infantry reckons with this.

460. When a crossing is successful, the main question then is, to rapidly gain room and freedom of action.

## F. MINE WARFARE.

461. Mine warfare is confined to long continued fighting for positions and permanent fortifications. Even then, it is the exception. Only absolute necessity of possession of tactically or strategically important points justifies mine warfare when the means above ground are insufficient. Always consider that mine warfare consumes forces, materiel, and time in an increased measure.

ms

462. By correct employment of suitable technical means, the nature of the ground and water conditions seldom prevent the execution of subterraneous attack and only in rare cases.

Explosion of mines is followed immediately by the assault.

463. The defender is frequently able to evade the hostile mine attack by changing the lines of his position. If that is impossible, the mine defense drives back the attacker above and below ground and creates a belt of craters difficult to push through.

Abandoned mines are demolished when the pursuers follow up; this is done by rear commands.

464. When the commander of the troops, after thorough consideration, decides on mine warfare, he quickly commences the construction of a regular mine net as deep as possible, and without superfluous minor works attempts to reach the desired point.

The battle under ground rests in one leading hand, generally that of the engineer battalion commander, who receives his orders from the division commander. Good communication by proper means is necessary, because rapid decisions are frequently made.

After an explosion of mine warfare, the side that can reach the leading points first has the advantage.

Labor forces, material, implements, and blasting supplies are placed in readiness and in sufficient quantities for the rapid progress of the works.

465. For the purpose of tranquilizing the troops it is important to find out whether and where, the enemy is constructing mines. For this purpose, there is the subterraneous listening service and the overground reconnaissance by observing from the trenches and by use of scouts. From the condition and the amount of earth which the enemy throws out at hidden points or carries away, conclusions are occasionally drawn as to his mining activity. From balloons or from elevated observation stations we ascertain if depressions in the terrain or cut out roads are being filled up in rear of the hostile lines, and whether trenches have been constructed there to serve to bring away the earth. Repeated photos taken from airplanes give excellent indications.

466. The available mine companies are generally reinforced by detachments of men from other units (miners, engine men, etc). The auxiliary men furnished by the infantry carry away the earth coming from the mines, work the pumps and winches, and carry on the listening service. During this listening service all noise and hammering, etc in the trenches ceases.

In addition to tactical measures (night operations against the hostile mine entrances, artillery and trench mortar fire to destroy them) the commander of the troops takes precautionary measures not only against our own but hostile explosions.

ms

www.ingramcontent.com/pod-product-compliance
Lightning Source LLC
LaVergne TN
LVHW070533110826
845147LV00017BA/977